Early American Cookery
"THE GOOD HOUSEKEEPER," 1841

Sarah Josepha Hale

With a New Introduction by
Janice (Jan) Bluestein Longone

DOVER PUBLICATIONS, INC.
Mineola, New York

Copyright

Published in Canada by General Publishing Company, Ltd., 30 Lesmill Road, Don Mills, Toronto, Ontario.
Published in the United Kingdom by Constable and Company, Ltd., 3 The Lanchesters, 162–164 Fulham Palace Road, London W6 9ER.

Bibliographical Note

This Dover edition, first published in 1996, is an unabridged republication of *The Good Housekeeper, or, the Way to Live Well, and to Be Well While We Live* (sixth edition), originally published by Otis, Broaders, and Company, Boston, in 1841 (first edition was 1839). A new Introduction has been written specially for this edition by Janice (Jan) Bluestein Longone.

Library of Congress Cataloging-in-Publication Data

Hale, Sarah Josepha Buell, 1788–1879.
  [Good housekeeper]
  Early American cookery = The good housekeeper / Sarah Josepha Hale ; with a new introduction by Janice (Jan) Bluestein Longone.
        p.   cm.
  Originally published: The good housekeeper, or The way to live well, and to be well while we live. 6th ed. Boston : Otis, Broaders, 1841.
    ISBN 0-486-29296-7 (pbk.)
    1. Cookery, American.   2. Home economics.   I. Title.
TX715.H1613   1996
641.5973—dc20   96-27374
                                                              CIP

Manufactured in the United States of America
Dover Publications, Inc., 31 East 2nd Street,
Mineola, N.Y. 11501

INTRODUCTION TO THE DOVER EDITION

Sarah Josepha Hale, the author of *The Good Housekeeper*, was a remarkable American. She was among the most influential women in nineteenth-century America and the arbiter of the nation's taste for a good portion of that century. Mrs. Hale achieved this position mainly through her longtime editorships, first of the *Ladies' Magazine* (1827–1836) and then, from 1837 to 1877, of *Godey's Lady's Book*, one of the most successful, important and often imitated of nineteenth-century publications. *Godey's* is considered the forerunner of modern women's magazines. It is difficult for us in the fast-paced news-overloaded late twentieth century to comprehend the influence of these early magazines. Eagerly sought and read, they shaped the lives of nineteenth-century Americans, both in the cities and on the farms.

Mrs. Hale's life and works have been part of the American fabric since 1827, when her first novel, *Northwood*, was published. Doctoral dissertations, books, numerous scholarly articles, voluminous stories and citations in the popular press, especially around Thanksgiving (for the public celebration of which she was in large part responsible), unceasingly bring her name to public attention. Feminist scholars and other historians continue to interpret and reinterpret—pro and con—her contributions to such diverse matters as civil rights and civil liberties; women's role in society, their civic and charitable responsibilities and, above all, their education; fashions in clothing and in the home; poetry and literature; magazine publishing and author's rights; and American patriotism and national unity. It is interesting to note that all of this has a very modern ring to it in that we still are concerned with many of these issues today.

Sarah Josepha Buell was born to Martha Whittlesey and Gordon Buell in Newport, New Hampshire, on October 24, 1788. Her father had been an officer serving under General Horatio Gates during the American Revolution. Returning home wounded and in ill health, he was always extremely proud of his role in American independence. His patriotism was clearly a major influence in Sarah's life. Her mother, with her unusual love of books and learning, had perhaps a greater influence. This combination of pride in America and belief in the importance of learning and education was the guiding principle of Sarah's long and productive life. She was one of four children. Her eldest brother, Charles, was lost at sea and her sister Martha died young of tuberculosis, both events perhaps leading to some of the social activism Sarah engaged in later in life. Her brother Horatio was her closest friend and companion, especially in matters of learning. Formal education

for women was not an option in those days. Thus, when Horatio went off to
Dartmouth, he literally shared his studies with Sarah, providing her with the
same textbooks and supervising her progress, so that upon his graduation,
she had received the equivalence of a college degree.

Sarah taught in a private school and then, upon her mother's early death in
1811, helped her father run the Rising Sun, a small inn in Newport. It was
there that she met, and in 1813 married, David Hale, a lawyer. Their marriage
appears to have been a most congenial one, with David encouraging Sarah in
her love of books and in her own writing. Sarah wrote, "We commenced, soon
after our marriage, a system of study and reading, which we pursued while he
lived. The hours allowed were from eight o'clock in the evening till ten; two
hours in the twenty-four; how I enjoyed those hours!"

Then, suddenly, in 1822, shortly before the birth of their fifth child, David
Hale died, leaving Sarah a widow with the necessity of raising and educating
her five children, the eldest only seven years old. After several attempts at a
new career, first as a milliner and then a poet (both professions partially
subsidized by David's fellow Masons), Sarah decided that her future lay in
full-time authorship. In 1827, her first novel, *Northwood*, was published to
much acclaim. Its success brought her an offer to edit the *Ladies' Magazine*,
which she developed into one of the first successful women's periodicals in
America.

Sarah edited the *Ladies' Magazine* first from Newport, then from Boston, to
which she moved in 1828, until 1837, when it was acquired by the publisher
Louis A. Godey of Philadelphia. She then became the editor of *Godey's
Lady's Book*, serving with distinction for forty years. She remained in Boston
while her youngest son was finishing his education at Harvard and then, in
1841, moved to Philadelphia, where she spent the rest of her life.

Many people today remember *Godey's* simply for its collectible color
fashion plates, but in its own day, it was an influential arbiter of social and
civic values, women's rights and responsibilities, literature, language,
intellectual life, music, home design and furnishing, fashion and home-
making and cooking. On the eve of the Civil War, *Godey's* was the most
widely read periodical in the United States, boasting 150,000 subscribers.

Sarah and Godey literally invented the American magazine, with an
American outlook and using American authors (and paying them well). In
the magazines she edited, Sarah rejected the then current practice of
"clipping," that is, reprinting, without permission or acknowledgment,
pieces from other journals, especially British publications. This was possible
as there were then no international copyright laws. Sarah championed and
promoted, tirelessly, American authors—especially women writers. She not
only published their works but promoted them in her editorials and book
reviews. Sarah published, among many others, works of Hawthorne, Irving,

Longfellow, Holmes, Emerson, Bryant, Whittier, Poe, Lydia Maria Child, Eliza Leslie, Lydia Sigourney and Harriet Beecher Stowe.

Her relationship with Edgar Allan Poe was an especially close one, beginning very early in his career. When Sarah's correspondence, covering fifty years of personal and editorial contact with writers whose works constitute American classics, was sold at auction in New York in 1917, it was a letter from Poe that attracted the greatest public attention. The letter included the line: "The price you mention—50 cts per page—will be amply sufficient; and I am exceedingly anxious to be ranked in your list of contributors." (Sarah's early work in encouraging American authors is still commemorated today. In 1956 friends of the Richards Library in Newport, New Hampshire, Sarah's birthplace, established an award in her honor. A medal is given each year to a prominent author associated with New England through work or residence. How appropriate that the list of modern recipients encompasses a Who's Who of twentieth-century authors equivalent to the Who's Who of nineteenth-century authors that Sarah published: Robert Frost, John P. Marquand, Archibald MacLeish, Catherine Drinker Bowen, John Hersey, Ogden Nash, Robert Lowell, John Kenneth Galbraith, Norman Cousins, May Sarton, Henry Steele Commager and Edwin Way Teale, among others.)

In addition to stories, serials, essays and poems, *Godey's* contained architectural patterns and plans; hand-colored fashion plates; music and dance compositions and instruction; sewing patterns; a "Ladies' Work Department" with detailed instructions for crocheting and other handiwork; advice on home furnishings, health, etiquette, home nursing, family medicine and consumer goods; science; cooking recipes; book reviews and an editorial section. Inclusion of the architectural patterns began in 1846 when *Godey's* encouraged private home ownership by establishing the first "own-your-own-home" department, Godey's Model Cottages. As for the fashion plates, *Godey's* published them against Sarah's own wishes, as she felt the clothing depicted was often either unhealthy or inconvenient for the modern American woman.

Above all, it was the book reviews and the editorials that Sarah used to endorse her position on many issues: the importance of women's education; property rights for women after marriage; daycare for children whose mothers had to work; greater job opportunities for women; fresh air, physical exercise, healthy clothing and good food to cure ills (such, perhaps, as the tuberculosis that killed her sister); encouragement of the training of women doctors, nurses and medical missionaries; playgrounds and open spaces for those in the cities; and a thousand other causes in which she believed. We should mention, though, that Sarah always clothed her preaching in "ladylike" garments and was neither in favor of women's suffrage nor of women competing with men in their own spheres.

Using her editorial position, and through her private efforts, Sarah accomplished many other good deeds in her long lifetime: She founded the Seaman's Aid Society (perhaps in honor of her brother who was lost at sea) and Homes for Sailors; she was instrumental in having President Lincoln mandate Thanksgiving as a national holiday; she worked tirelessly to raise funds for the completion of the Bunker Hill Monument to honor soldiers of the American Revolution, and to have George Washington's Mount Vernon preserved for posterity. She was influential in the founding of Vassar College, the first major school of higher education for women in America; she worked with Mary Lyon of Mt. Holyoke and Emma Willard, the pioneer educator of young women. She encouraged and publicized Catherine Beecher's American Women's Educational Association, which trained women as teachers for western settlements.

Busy as she was, Sarah still found time to write prolifically. She authored novels, poems, short stories, essays, plays, children's books, etiquette manuals and cookbooks and edited anthologies and the collected letters of famous literary figures. Among her novels *Northwood, Liberia, Keeping House and House Keeping* and *Boarding Out* are her best known. Her most famous poem is "Mary Had a Little Lamb." She edited the letters of Madame de Sévigné and of Lady Mary Wortley Montagu. Sarah's book on etiquette, *Manners: or, Happy Homes and Good Society All the Year Round,* went through at least three editions. Her most lasting contribution, perhaps, was her *Woman's Record; A Biographical Dictionary of all Distinguished Women from the Creation to A.D. 1850 . . . With Selections from Feminine Writers of Every Age.* This massive compilation, first published in 1853, had more than 1000 pages and was illustrated with hundreds of portraits. It was revised and enlarged in subsequent editions until 1870 and is still used as a reference book.

But it is Sarah Josepha Hale's cookbooks that we want particularly to address here. In addition to *The Good Housekeeper,* Sarah wrote several other cookbooks. All of them went through many printings, often with variant titles, appearing as the *Ladies' New Book of Cookery, Mrs. Hale's New Cookbook, The New Household Receipt Book, Mrs. Hale's Receipts for the Millions* and *The Way to Live Well.* In addition, it is quite fitting that Sarah revised and prepared for the American market one of the most important contemporary English cookbooks, Eliza Acton's *Modern Cookery in All Its Branches.* Sarah's cookbooks went through more than thirty editions or printings in America, and were also published in England.

When Sarah wrote *The Good Housekeeper* in 1839, the number of original American cookbooks published was quite small, fewer than thirty. Thus, Sarah felt that there was a need for a new *American* cookbook, following certain principles. She explains that those who wanted to learn the art of "good living" could turn to the *Cook's Oracle* (by Dr. William Kitchiner) while those who wanted to learn about "cheap living" could consult the *Frugal Housewife* (by Lydia Maria Child). Sarah's aim was "to select and combine the excellences of these two systems, at the same time keeping in view the important object of preserving health, and thus teach *how to live well, and to be well while we live."*

Sarah does this quite nicely. This book is full of information about cooking and health and economy, yet it always takes pains to be concerned with taste and comfort. Many of the recipes offer personal, savory touches that result in delicious dishes. The Rich Apple Pudding, the Squash Pie, the Heart Cakes and the Cream Short Cakes would honor any table. Not all the recipes, of course, can be followed by the modern cook. Few will want to make the Mock Turtle Soup, but the Old Pease Soup is easily accomplished. Sarah's discussion of the role of bread in family life and her vindication of meat-eating make intriguing reading today.

A splendid way to savor Mrs. Hale's cooking might be to prepare a Thanksgiving dinner based upon the one she describes in *Northwood*.

> And now for our Thanksgiving dinner.
> The roasted turkey took precedence on this occasion, being placed at the head of the table; and well did it become its lordly station, sending forth the rich odor of its savory stuffing, and finely covered with the froth of the basting. At the foot of the board, a sirloin of beef, flanked on either side by a leg of pork and loin of mutton, seemed placed as a bastion to defend the innumerable bowls of gravy and plates of vegetables disposed in that quarter. A goose and pair of ducklings occupied side stations on the table; the middle being graced . . . by that rich burgomaster of the provisions, called a chicken pie. This pie, which is wholly formed of the choicest parts of fowls, enriched and seasoned with a profusion of butter and pepper, and covered with an excellent puff paste is, like the celebrated pumpkin pie, an indispensable part of a good and true Yankee Thanksgiving.
> Plates of pickles, preserves and butter, and all the necessaries for increasing the seasoning of the viands to the demands of each palate, filled the interstices on the table, leaving hardly sufficient room for the plates of the company, a wine glass and two tumblers for each, with a slice of wheat bread lying on one of the inverted tumblers. A side table was literally loaded with the preparations for the second course.
> There was a huge plum pudding, custards and pies of every name and description known in Yankee land; yet the pumpkin pie occupied the most distinguished niche. There were also several kinds of rich cake, and a variety of sweetmeats and fruits.

Recipes for each of the dishes named can be found in the historic American cookbook you have in your hand. Read this book for its recipes, of course, but also savor it as a slice of American history—a picture of a woman and a world.

Sarah retired from *Godey's* in 1877 and continued writing until her death at ninety-one on April 30, 1879.

Earlier in her life, Sarah had written that she had entered into her literary life not because she wanted fame and fortune, but because she needed to support and educate her children. How proud she must have been of them. Both her daughters studied to be teachers and graduated from Emma Willard's School in Troy, New York. Sarah Josepha (b. 1820) taught in a private school in Georgia for a number of years before opening her own successful and fashionable Boarding and Day School for Young Ladies on Rittenhouse Square in Philadelphia. She never married, and died at her desk on May 3, 1863. Frances Ann (b. 1819) married Dr. Lewis Boudinet Hunter, a naval surgeon. Sarah spent the last years of her life in their home, surrounded by adoring grandchildren. Her oldest son, David Emerson (b. 1815), graduated from West Point and died young in the service of his country in 1839. Her youngest son, William George, graduated from Harvard and practiced law in Virginia before moving to Texas, where he became renowned for handling the old Spanish claims that immediately flooded the courts of Texas upon its separation from Mexico. No history of Texas could be written without including the invaluable role played by William Hale.

Sarah's middle son, Horatio, a renowned ethnologist and linguist, conducted the pioneer investigation into the customs, languages and dialects of North American Indians, both in the United States and in Canada. For these contributions he was described as "the greatest scholar in Canada in the nineteenth century."

In an autobiographical essay in her book *Woman's Record,* Sarah had indicated that what she wanted to do with her life was "to promote the reputation of my own sex, and do something for my own country." She succeeded beyond her wildest possible dreams.

I would like to thank Dover Publications for its commitment to publishing milestones of American culinary history, of which this is the *fourth volume.* Dover has wisely chosen to reprint a later edition of *The Good Housekeeper* because it includes the informative preface to the Second Edition, giving us insight into its printing history and a bit more of Sarah Josepha Hale's philosophy.

Janice (Jan) Bluestein Longone
The Wine and Food Library
Ann Arbor, Michigan
June 1996

NOTES

1. Those interested in further information on Sarah Josepha Hale can consult numerous sources. She is chronicled in most major reference works on famous Americans, notable women and major writers. Of published material solely on Sarah Hale, the following are especially useful:

Entrikin, Isabelle Webb. *Sarah Josepha Hale and Godey's Lady's Book.* Philadelphia: Lancaster, 1946.

Finley, Ruth E. *The Lady of Godey's: Sarah Josepha Hale.* Philadelphia: Lippincott, 1932.

Fryatt, Norma R. *Sarah Josepha Hale: The Life and Times of a Nineteenth-Century Career Woman.* New York: Hawthorn Books, Inc., 1957.

Hale, Sarah Josepha. *Woman's Record: or, A Biographical Dictionary of all Distinguished Women from the Creation to A.D. 1850.* New York: Harper and Brothers, 1853.

Hoffman, Nicole Tonkovich. *"Legacy* Profile: Sarah Josepha Hale." *Legacy* 7 (Fall 1990): pp.47–55.

Okker, Patricia. *Our Sister Editors: Sarah J. Hale and the Tradition of Nineteenth-Century Women Editors.* Athens, Georgia, & London: The University of Georgia Press, 1995.

Rogers, Sherbrooke. *Sarah Josepha Hale: A New England Pioneer, 1788–1879.* Grantham, NH: Thompson & Rutter, 1985.

2. The others are: *The First American Cookbook: A Facsimile of "American Cookery," 1796,* Amelia Simmons [1984; ISBN 0-486-24710-4]; *The Virginia Housewife* (1869), Mary Randolph [1993; ISBN 0-486-27772-0]; and *Boston Cooking School Cook Book: A Reprint of the 1884 Classic,* Mary J. Lincoln [1996; ISBN 0-486-29196-0].

Early American Cookery

"THE GOOD HOUSEKEEPER," 1841

TO

EVERY AMERICAN WOMAN,

WHO WISHES TO PROMOTE THE

HEALTH, COMFORT, AND PROSPERITY

OF HER FAMILY,

THIS BOOK IS

DEDICATED.

PREFACE TO THE SECOND EDITION.

THE first edition of the Good Housekeeper (2000 copies) was nearly disposed of in the space of a month after its publication, and large orders for the work have been since received. These marks of public approbation show that our system of domestic management meets the wants and wishes of the community. This was our aim—to prepare a Manual of Cookery which should, by its cheapness, be accessible to every family, and by its clearness, simplicity, and adaptation to the human constitution and tastes of civilized life, be practical for all classes—for the rich and poor, the dweller in the city, and the country household.

By crowding the text, a few more receipts have been given in this edition, chiefly in relation to preserving meats and preparing gravies, mixed spices and flavored vinegars. These are selected from " The Cook and Housewife's Manual," a work ostensibly by " Mrs. Margaret Dods," but said to have been prepared by Sir Walter Scott. The opening chapters, which give a graphic and most humorous description of the " Cleikum Club," their experiments in cookery, and lectures on culinary matters, bear internal evidence of the style of the great novelist. His visit to Paris seems to have opened a new world of tastes to his palate, and his admiration of French cookery is very apparent. He echoes the sentiment of Dr. King with great warmth :

> " Muse, sing the man that did to Paris go,
> That he might taste their soups, and sauces know."

It is generally admitted that the French excel in the economy of their cooking. By studying the appropriate flavors for every dish, they contrive to dress all the broken pieces of meats, and make a variety of dishes from vegetables at a small expense.

Next to the knowledge of the differences in the human constitution, and the nature of the food proper for man, this study of flavors and art of recooking to advantage is to be prized by the good housekeeper. Every family who has a garden spot should cultivate those vegetables and herbs which are requisite for seasoning—horseradish, onions, celery, mustard, capsicum, (red pepper,) sage, summer savory, mint, &c. &c. are easily raised. These, if rightly prepared, will be sufficient for all common culinary purposes, and a little care and study will enable the housekeeper to flavor her meats, gravies, and vegetables in the best manner.

Bear in mind that in preparing food, three things are to be united, the promotion of health, the study of economy, and the gratification of taste.

Boston, November 1, 1839.

PREFACE TO THE FIRST EDITION.

It has been the aim of the author, in the following pages, to point out as clearly as the limits of the work permitted, the nature of the different kinds of aliment provided by the wise and benevolent Creator for the sustenance of his rational creatures, and to show the best methods of preparation now understood.

Foreigners say that our climate is unhealthy; that the Americans have, generally, thin forms, sallow complexions, and bad teeth.

Is it not most likely that those defects are incurred, in part, if not wholly, because the diet and modes of living are unsuitable to the climate, and consequently to the health of the people?

Could public attention be drawn to this important subject sufficiently to have a reform in a few points—such as using *animal food* to excess, eating *hot bread*, and swallowing our meals with steam-engine rapidity, the question of climate might more easily be settled.

This little work is intended to show the rich how they may preserve their health, and yet enjoy the bounties of Providence; and teach the poor that frugal management which will make their homes the abode of comfort. Such rational and Christian views of domestic economy have never before been enforced in a treatise on housekeepng; and the writer flatters herself that this will be well received. The book has been several years in contemplation; various circumstances have retarded the publication, but the times seemed now to call for its appearance. May it do good, is the sincere wish of the

AUTHOR.

Boston, September 1, 1839.

TABLE OF WEIGHTS AND MEASURES.

By which persons not having scales and weights at hand may readily measure the articles wanted to form any receipt, without the trouble of weighing. Allowance to be made for an extraordinary dryness or moisture of the article weighed or measured.

WEIGHT AND MEASURE.

Wheat flour..............one pound is ....one quart.
Indian meal..............one pound, two ounces, is...one quart.
Butter, when soft.........one pound is...............one quart.
Loaf sugar, broken.......one pound is...............one quart.
White sugar, powdered....one pound, one ounce, is ...one quart
Best brown sugar.........one pound, two ounces, is...one quart.
Eggs ....ten eggs are ....one pound
Flour....................eight quarts are ....one peck.
Flour....................four pecks are ....one bushel.

LIQUIDS.

Sixteen large table-spoonfuls are ....half a pint.
Eight large table-spoonfuls are ....one gill.
Four large table-spoonfuls are ....half a gill.
Two gills are ....half a pint.
Two pints are ....one quart.
Four quarts are ....one gallon.
A common-sized tumbler holds ....half a pint.
A common-sized wine-glass ....half a gill.
Twenty-five drops are equal to one tea-spoonful.

CONTENTS.

---�»◦●◉●◦◄---

8

CONTENTS.

10 CONTENTS.

THE GOOD HOUSEKEEPER.

CHAPTER I.

INTRODUCTORY.

Bodily health, satisfied appetite, and peace of mind, are great promoters of individual morality and public tranquillity.—Dr. Combe.

The main object of those who have prepared works on cookery, has been to teach the art of *good living,* or of *cheap living ;*—the "Cook's Oracle" is one of the best examples for the first purpose, the "Frugal Housewife" of the last.

My aim is to select and combine the excellences of these two systems, at the same time keeping in view the important object of preserving health, and thus teach *how to live well, and to be well while we live.*

The physiology of digestion and the principles of dietetics, as laid down and explained by Dr. Andrew Combe, of Edinburgh, form the basis of my plan, which will inculcate temperance in all things, but rarely enforce total abstinence from any thing which the Creator has sanctioned, as proper food for mankind.

I follow chiefly in the system of Dr. Combe, because, though I have examined many popular works on Diet, Health, &c. and have found much to commend, and some things to adopt from these writers, yet he defines, with most clearness and precision, those rules of living, which my own experience has taught me are good and judicious. Indeed, in most cases, even when I may quote the language of Dr. Combe, I still write what I know to be true.

I have been a housekeeper, both in the country and the city, and have had a practical knowledge of those rules of domestic economy which I shall recommend. And I have brought up a family of children, without the loss, or hardly the sickness, of one of them during infancy and childhood. I can, therefore, claim some experience in a successful manner of managing the health and constitution of the young.

As our bodily health, and, consequently, our happiness and usefulness in domestic and social life, depend very much on the proper quantity of food we eat, and the time and circumstances under which it is taken, I shall give a few hints on these subjects, before laying down rules for the preparation and quality of the food.

TIMES OF TAKING FOOD.—Nature has fixed no particular hours for eating. When the mode of life is uniform, it is of great importance to adopt fixed hours ; when it is irregular, we ought to be guided by the real wants of the system as dictated by appetite.

A strong laboring man, engaged in hard work, will require food oftener and in larger quantities than an indolent or sedentary man.

As a general rule, about five hours should elapse between one meal and another—longer, if the mode of life be indolent ; shorter, if it be very active.

When dinner is delayed seven or eight hours after breakfast, some slight refreshment should be taken between.

Young persons when growing fast, require more food and at shorter intervals, than those do who have attained maturity.

Children under seven years of age, usually need food every three hours ; a piece of bread will be a healthy lunch, and a child seldom eats bread to excess.

During the first months of infancy, there can be no set times of giving nourishment. Different constitutions require different management. The best rule is to satisfy the real wants of the child, but never tempt it to take food to still its crying from pain when it is not hungry.

Those persons who eat a late supper should not take breakfast till one or two hours after rising. Those who dine late, and eat nothing afterwards, require breakfast soon after rising.

Persons of a delicate constitution should never exercise much before breakfast.

If exposure of any kind is to be incurred in the morning, breakfast should always be taken previously. The system is more susceptible of infection and of the influence of cold, miasma, &c., in the morning before eating, than at any other time.

Those who walk early will find great benefit from taking a cracker or some little nourishment before going out.

Never go into a room of a morning, where a person is sick with a fever, before you have taken nourishment of some kind—a cup of coffee, at least.

In setting out early to travel, a light breakfast before starting should always be taken; it is a great protection against cold, fatigue and exhaustion.

In boarding schools for the young and growing, early breakfast is an indispensable condition to health. Children should not be kept without food in the morning till they are faint and weary.

Never eat a hearty supper just before retiring to rest.

It is injurious to eat when greatly heated or fatigued. It would very much conduce to the health of laboring men if they could rest fifteen or twenty minutes before dinner.

PROPER QUANTITY OF FOOD.—As a general fact, those who can obtain sufficient food, eat much more than is required for their sustenance.

Nearly one half of the diseases and deaths occurring during the first two years of existence, are owing to mismanagement and errors in diet.

Children should never be fed or tempted to eat when appetite is satisfied; and grown persons should also be careful of eating beyond that point.

The indigestion so much complained of, and which causes so many disorders and sufferings in the human system, is a wise provision of nature, to prevent the repletion which would otherwise ensue, when too much food is taken.

The power of digestion is limited to the amount of gastric juice the stomach is capable of providing; exercise, in the open air, promotes the secretion of the gastric juice.

It is a good and safe rule to proportion our meals to the amount of exercise we have taken; if that exercise has been in the open air, there is less danger of excess. The delicate lady, who scarcely walks abroad, should live very sparingly, or she will be troubled with nervousness, headache, and all the horrors of indigestion.

Young persons, when growing, should have plenty of food; if they are active and healthy, and the food is of a proper kind and well prepared, there is little danger of their taking too much. But never tempt their appetites by delicacies, when plain food is not relished.

When the growth is attained, and active exercises are in a great measure abandoned—as is the case with females, particularly,—then be very careful to regulate the appetite, and never take such a quantity of food at a time, as to oppress or disturb the stomach. Remember that food which does not digest cannot nourish the system, but rather weakens it.

Variety of food is chiefly dangerous because it tempts to excess; otherwise it is beneficial. The gastric juice acts more easily where the contents of the stomach are of different kinds of food mixed together. Let no person think he is *certainly temperate* because he eats of but *one* dish. It is more hurtful to take too much of that one, than though he had eaten the same quantity of several.

Generally speaking, when food does not agree with the stomach, it is a sign that too much has been taken.

WHAT IS THE PROPER FOOD OF MAN?—No certain rules can be given respecting the kind of food to be taken. The same diet which is healthful for an adult will be injurious for a child. The stimulating animal diet which in winter is necessary for a laboring man, would be destructive to an inactive and excitable man during the summer months.

Food should be adapted to the age, constitution, state of health and mode of life of the individual; to the climate, and the season of the year.

The milk of the mother ought in every instance to constitute the food of an infant, unless such an arrangement is impracticable. After the child is weaned, fresh cow's milk in which a small portion of soft water has been mingled, and sometimes a little sugar, with a small quantity of crust of bread softened, is usually the most healthy food; but this should be varied by occasional meals of gruel, arrow-root, or sago, and if the child is delicate and shows signs of acidity or flatulence, then a preparation of weak chicken broth or beef tea, freed from fat, and thickened with soft boiled rice, may be given.

The same kind of food ought to be continued, with the addition of good bread, (and potatoes, when well cooked, seem as healthy food nearly as bread,) till the appearance of the " eye teeth;" when these are fairly through, a portion of soft-boiled egg, and occasionally a little meat, the lean part, well cooked and not highly seasoned, may be given.

There is great danger of over-feeding young children with animal food. If given too early, and too freely, it irritates the system, and greatly aggravates the diseases of infancy.

Ripe fruits should never be given to children till they have teeth, and unripe fruits ought never to be eaten.

During childhood and early youth, the breakfast and supper should consist principally of bread and milk, ripe fruits and vegetable food; it will be sufficient to allow a portion of animal food with the dinner.

Fish, chicken, and other white meats are best for children. Fat pork is nearly indigestible for the young and delicate, and ought never to be eaten by them.

Pastry, rich cakes, plum-puddings, hot short-cakes, and all the family of fried cakes, are the most generally indigestible of any kinds of food. These should rarely be eaten, except by the strong and actively employed, and sparingly even by those.

In truth, there are few articles of diet which a person in health, and leading a very active life, may not eat without feeling much inconvenience; still a preference should be given, as far as possible, to such kinds of food as are most in accordance with the natural constitution. A phlegmatic temperament requires a mild, nutritious diet, but not the same amount of animal food as may be needed by the sanguine, which inclines to great physical activity. Those in whom the brain and nervous system predominate, should avoid a stimulating diet, unless they are in the habit of taking considerable muscular exercise. If it be the wish to rouse a phlegmatic organization to greater activity, then use a richer diet, more animal food—but be sure and take exercise at the same time, or it will prove highly injurious. The natural temperament may be essentially altered by diet and exercise.

Rich soups are injurious to the dyspeptic. Much liquid food is rarely beneficial for adults; but a small quantity of plain, nourishing soup is an economic and healthy beginning of a family dinner.

Meats should always be sufficiently cooked. It is a savage custom to eat meat in a half-raw-half-roasted state, and only a very strong stomach can digest it.

Rich gravies should be avoided, especially in the summer season.

Butter, when new and sweet, is nutritious, and, in our climate, generally healthy; during the winter, when made very salt, it is not a good article of diet.

Pepper, ginger, and most of the condiments, are best during summer; they are productions of hot climates, which shows them to be most appropriate for the hot season. On the other hand, fat beef, bacon, and those kinds of food we denominate "hearty," should be most freely used during cold weather,

The diet should always be more spare, with a larger proportion of vegetables and ripe fruits, during summer. Fruits are most wholesome in their appropriate season. The skins, stones, and seeds, are indigestible.

Food should never be eaten when it is hot—bread is very unhealthy when eaten in this way.

Eat slowly. One of the most usual causes of dyspepsia among our business men, arises from the haste in which they swallow their food without sufficiently chewing it, and then hurry away to their active pursuits. In England very little business is transacted after dinner. There ought to be, at least, one hour of quiet after a full meal, from those pursuits which tax the brain as well as those which exercise the muscles.

WHAT SHALL WE DRINK?—Why, water—that is a safe drink for all constitutions and all ages,—provided persons only use it when they are naturally thirsty. But do not drink heartily of cold water when heated or greatly fatigued. A cup of warm tea will better allay the thirst, and give a feeling of comfort to the stomach, which water will not.

Toast and water, common beer, soda water, and other liquids of a similar kind, if they agree with the stomach, may be used freely without danger.

Fermented liquors, such as porter, ale, and wine, if used at all as a drink, should be very sparingly taken.

Distilled spirituous liquors should never be considered drinkable—they may be necessary, sometimes, as a medicine, but never, never consider them a necessary item in house-keeping. So important does it appear to me to dispense entirely with distilled spirits, as an article of domestic use, that I have not allowed a drop to enter into any of the recipes contained in this book.

As the primary effect of fermented liquors, cider, wine, &c., is to stimulate the nervous system, and quicken the circulation, these should be utterly prohibited to children and persons of a quick temperament. In truth, unless prescribed by the physician, it would be best to abstain entirely from their use.

Most people drink too much, because they drink too fast. A wine-glass of water, sipped slowly, will quench the thirst as effectually as a pint swallowed at a draught. When too much is taken at meals, especially at dinner, it hinders digestion. Better drink little during the meal, and then, if thirsty an hour or two afterwards, more. The practice of taking a cup of tea or coffee soon after dinner is a good one, if the beverage be not drank too strong or too hot.

Dyspeptic people should be careful to take but a small quantity of drink. Children require more, in proportion to their food than adults. But it is very injurious to them to allow a habit of continual drinking as you find in some children. It greatly weakens the stomach, and renders them irritable and peevish.

The morning meal requires to be lighter and of a more fluid nature than any other. Children should always, if possible to be obtained, take milk—as a substitute, during the winter, good gruel with bread, or water, sweetened with molasses, is healthy.   Never give children tea, coffee, or chocolate with their meals.

Coffee affords very little nourishment, and is apt, if drank strong, to occasion tremors of the nerves.   It is very bad for bilious constitutions.   The calm, phlegmatic temperament can bear it.   With a good supply of cream and sugar, drank in moderation, by those who exercise much and take considerable solid food, it may be used without much danger.

Strong green tea relaxes the tone of the stomach, and excites the nervous system.   Persons of delicate constitution are almost sure to be injured by it.   Black tea is much less deleterious.   If used with milk and sugar, it may be considered healthy for most people.

Chocolate, when it agrees with the constitution, is very nutritious and healthy.   But it seldom can be used steadily except by aged persons who are very active.   It agrees best with persons of phlegmatic temperament; and is more healthy in the winter season than during warm weather.

No kind of beverage should be taken hot—it injures the teeth and impairs digestion.

I have now given those general rules and hints in regard to diet, which will greatly preserve the health and promote the comfort of those who follow them.   Particular directions and peculiar constitutions cannot be considered or recorded in this book, which is rather intended as a manual for those who require to be instructed how to remain *well*, than for the *sick*.   Though for these, the plan of diet here recommended, if strictly followed, will be a great relief—in most cases, a radical cure.

We are now to give all necessary directions for the preparation of food in accordance with these rules for health and real enjoyment.   I trust that every woman will agree in sentiment with the lady in Milton's Comus—

> " That which is not good (beneficial) is not delicious
> To a well-governed and wise appetite."

CHAPTER II.

BREAD.

Importance of good bread—Diet proper for mankind—Proofs that a
mixed diet is the best—Advantages of taking a portion of animal
food—Flour—Bread—Making Yeast—Hints on the economy of
bread making, &c.

THE art of making *good bread* I consider the most important one in cookery, and shall therefore give it the first place in the "Good Housekeeper." Not that I believe bread to contain the "quintessence of beef, mutton, veal, venison," or that an exclusive vegetable diet is best for mankind.

There has been, of late years, much said and written respecting the benefits of adhering to a strict vegetable diet, and many excellent people are sadly perplexed about their duty in this matter, and whether they ought to give up animal food entirely. As I profess to make my book a manual for those who wish to preserve their health, as well as prepare their food in the most judicious manner, I will here give a brief sketch of the reasons which induce me to recommend a mixed diet, *bread, meat, vegetables and fruits, as the best, the only right regimen for the healthy.*

It is an established truth in physiology, that man is omnivorous*—that is, constituted to eat almost every kind of food which, separately, nourishes other animals. His teeth and stomach are formed to digest and masticate flesh, fish, and all farinaceous and vegetable substances—he can eat and digest these even in a raw state; but it is necessary to

* Some determined advocates of the vegetable system maintain, that the teeth and stomach of the monkey correspond, in structure, very closely with that of man, yet it lives on fruits—therefore, if man followed nature, he would live on fruits and vegetables. But though the anatomical likeness between man and monkeys is striking, yet it is not complete; the difference may be and doubtless is precisely that which makes a difference of diet necessary to nourish and develope their dissimilar natures. Those who should live as the monkeys do would most closely resemble them.

perfect them for his nourishment in the most healthy manner, that they be prepared by cooking—that is, softened by the use of fire and water.

Such is the evidence of nature to the suitableness of a mixed diet for the human race. The appointments of the Creator correspond with the structure of man. At the first, indeed, he was limited : " Behold, I have given you every herb bearing seed, which is upon the face of all the earth, and every tree in the which is the fruit of a tree yielding seed ; to you it shall be for meat," was the language of God to Adam.

There is no intimation that any other diet was used for nearly seventeen hundred years. But this vegetable food did not nourish and develop the human faculties. The physical propensities must have had an almost overwhelming dominion, and if the intellectual powers were developed, they must have been made subservient to the basest animal passions, for the whole earth was filled with violence, and men were utterly corrupt and wicked. The moral sentiments seem scarcely to have been felt or cultivated at all. And does not the same character, that is, the predominance of the physical over the intellectual and moral, mark even now, in a considerable degree, every nation where, either from climate, custom or condition, the mass of the people are compelled to subsist chiefly on vegetable food ?

When, after the destruction of the old world, Noah and his family came forth from the ark, and God assured him that, while the earth continued, the race should not be again plunged in such utter ruin, what new agent of human improvement and civilization was brought to the aid of mankind? We are told of none excepting a change in their diet ;—the permission, or command rather, to Noah to use animal food. " Every moving thing that liveth shall be meat for you; even as the green herb have I given you all things. But flesh with the life thereof, which is the blood thereof, shall ye not eat."

Such was the Creator's arrangement, when he had determined that the character and condition of his rational creatures should go on improving, till the whole earth should be peopled, and all be filled with the knowledge of the Lord.

And here we may remark, that the tribe or nation, who violates the express command of God, to separate the flesh from the blood and not to use the latter, and eats raw meat, never improves in character or condition. In truth, the command includes the rudiments of cookery, the preparation of food by the aid of fire; and till this is the constant habit of the community, men are savages.

If it be asked why, when flesh as a part of man's diet was so necessary to his well-being, was it not appointed him at the beginning,—Solve me this question—Why was the earth a progressive creation, which, as the researches of philosophers have conclusively proved, required thousands of ages to bring to its present state of mineral, vegetable and animal perfection? That same answer is true for both— it was the purpose of God to show forth his power, wisdom and goodness in a progressive rather than an instantaneous perfecting of his works.

In this respect, man is in harmony with the sphere he inhabits.

But one thing is certain; since the appointment of flesh as a part of man's diet, no instance is recorded of its having been prohibited by divine authority. Intoxicating drinks have been forbidden to certain individuals; but from the time of righteous Abraham, who dressed a calf the better to entertain his angel visitors, till the coming of John, " whose meat was locust and wild honey," no servant of God has been confined to a vegetable diet. The prophet who was fed by his express command, had " bread and flesh" twice each day.

In strict accordance with this theory, which makes a portion of animal food necessary to develop and sustain the human constitution, in its most perfect state of physical, intellectual and moral strength and beauty, we know that now in every country, where a mixed diet is habitually used, as in the temperate climates, there the greatest improvement of the race is to be found, and the greatest energy of character. It is that portion of the human family, who have the means of obtaining this food at least once a day, who now hold dominion over the earth. Forty thousand of the beef-fed British govern and control ninety millions of the rice-eating natives of India.

In every nation on earth the *rulers*, the men of power, whether princes or priests, almost invariably use a portion of animal food. The people are often compelled, either from poverty or policy, to abstain.—Whenever the time shall arrive that every *peasant* in Europe is able to "put his pullet in the pot," even of a Sunday, a great improvement will have taken place in his character and condition; when he can have a portion of animal food, properly cooked, once each day, he will soon become a *man*.

In our own country, the beneficial effects of a generous diet, in developing and sustaining the energies of a whole nation, are clearly evident. The severe and unremitting labors of every kind, which were requisite to subdue and obtain dominion of a wilderness world, could not have been done by a half-starved, suffering people. A larger quantity and better quality of food were necessary here than would have supplied men in the old countries, where less action of body and mind are permitted.

Still, there is great danger of excess in all indulgences of the appetites; even when a present benefit may be obtained, this danger should never be forgotten. The tendency in our country has been to excess in animal food. The advocates of the vegetable diet system had good cause for denouncing this excess, and the indiscriminate use of flesh. It was, and now is, frequently given to young children—infants before they have teeth, which is a sin against nature, which often costs the life of the poor little sufferer; it is eaten too freely by the sedentary and delicate; and to make it worse still, it is eaten, often in a half-cooked state, and swallowed without sufficient chewing. All these things are wrong, and ought to be reformed.

I hope "The Good Housekeeper" will do something towards enlightening public opinion on the proper kinds of food and the proper manner of preparing it. These subjects have never been sufficiently considered. Many, probably most, of the receipts now in use, have been the result of chance or the whim of a depraved appetite. But as the spirit of inquiry is abroad, searching out abuses of all kinds, let us hope that the abuses of the good things God has so bounteously given us will not be suffered to go unreproved.

When women are thoroughly instructed in physiology and the natural laws which govern the human constitution, in chemistry and in domestic economy, then we may expect that desideratum of Doctor Johnson—a cookery book on philosophical principles.

And now we will turn to the subject of *bread*, and describe minutely the best practical manner of preparation at present understood.

Flour.—The first requisite for *good bread* is that the flour or meal be good. Wheat is always better for being washed; if it be at all injured by smut, it is not fit for food unless it be thoroughly washed. In the country this is easily done.

Put the grain in a clean tub, a bushel at a time; fill the tub with water, and stir the whole up from the bottom, briskly, with your hand, or a stick. Pour off the water and fill it with clean till the water ceases to be colored or dirty. Two or three waters usually are sufficient. Finish the washing quickly as possible, so as not to soak the grain; then spread it thinly on a large, strong sheet, (it is best to keep a coarse unbleached sheet solely for this purpose, if you wash your grain,) laid on clean boards in the sun, or where the sun and air can be freely admitted. Stir the grain with your hand every two or three hours; it will dry in a day, if the weather be fair.

Fresh-ground flour makes the best and sweetest bread. If you live in the vicinity of a mill, never have more than one or two bushels ground into flour at a time.

A bushel of good, clear wheat will make fifty-six pounds of flour, beside the bran and middlings.

If you purchase flour by the barrel or sack, be careful to ascertain that it is good and pure. In Europe, flour is often adulterated, that is, mixed with other substances, to swell its bulk and weight. *Whiting, ground stones, and bones, and plaster of Paris,* are the ingredients chiefly used. To be sure, none of these things are absolutely poisonous; but they are injurious, and no one wants them in bread. In our country we think such deceptions are seldom attempted, still it may be well to know how to detect the least bad matter in flour.

To discover *whiting*, dip the ends of the fore-finger and thumb into sweet oil, and take up a small quantity of flour between them. If it be pure, you may freely rub the fingers together for any length of time, it will not become sticky, and the substance will turn nearly black; if whiting be mixed with the flour, a few times rubbing turns it into putty, but its color is very little changed.

To detect stone dust or plaster of Paris—drop the juice of lemon or a little sharp vinegar on a small quantity of flour; if adulterated, an immediate commotion or effervescence takes place; if pure, it will remain at rest. Another quick, easy and pretty sure method of trial is to take a handful of flour and squeeze it very tightly for a minute— if it be good and pure, when you open your hand, the flour will remain in a lump, in the form you have given it, even the grains and wrinkles of the skin of the hand will be visible—you may place it on the table without breaking; but if it contain foreign substances, it will not adhere thus, but crumble and fall almost immediately.

Sour or musty flour may be easily known by the smell. Such damaged stuff can never make good, healthy bread, though public bakers, it is said, often prefer to use it, because it is cheapest, and they know methods of preparation by which they can produce light and white bread from this damaged flour. The bread is, to be sure, nearly tasteless, and it cannot be equally nourishing as good flour would make; but if it looks white, it will *sell*. Those who bake their own bread have the opportunity of knowing that it is made of good ingredients; and if they make it after the following recipe they may be sure of good bread.

MAKING BREAD.

A large family will, probably, use a bushel of flour weekly; but we will take the proper quantity for a family of four or five persons.

Take *twenty-one quarts* of flour, put it into a kneading trough or earthen pan which is well glazed, and large enough to hold double the quantity of flour. Make a deep, round hole in the centre of the flour, and pour into it *half a pint* of brewer's yeast, or the thick sediment from home-brewed beer—the last, if good, is to be preferred. In either case the yeast must be mixed with a pint of milk-warm water, and well stirred before it is poured in. Then with a spoon stir into this liquid, gradually, so much of the surrounding flour as will make it like thin batter; sprinkle this over with dry flour, till it is covered entirely. Then cover the trough or pan with a warm cloth, and set it by the fire in winter, and where the sun is shining in summer. This process is called "setting the sponge." The object is to give strength and character to the ferment by communicating the quality of *leaven* to a small portion of the flour, which will then be easily extended to the whole. *Setting sponge* is a measure of wise precaution—for if the yeast does not rise and ferment in the middle of the flour, it shows that the yeast is not good; the batter can then be removed, without wasting much of the flour, and another sponge set with better yeast.

Let the sponge stand till the batter has swelled and risen so as to form cracks in the covering of flour; then scatter over it two table-spoonfuls of fine salt, and begin to form the mass into dough by pouring in, by degrees, as much warm water as is necessary to mix with the flour. *Twenty-one quarts of flour* will require about *four quarts of water.* It will be well to prepare rather more; soft water is much the best; it should in summer be warm as new milk; during winter, it ought to be somewhat warmer, as flour is a cold, heavy substance.

Add the water by degrees to the flour, mix them with your hand, till the whole mass is incorporated; it must then be worked most thoroughly, moulded over and over, and kneaded with your clenched hands, till it becomes so perfectly smooth and light as well as stiff, that not a particle will adhere to your hands. Remember that you cannot have good bread, light and white, unless you give the dough a thorough kneading.—Then make the dough into a lump in the middle of the trough or pan, and dust it over with flour to prevent its adhering to the vessel. Cover it with a warm cloth, and in the winter the vessel should be placed near the fire. It now undergoes a further fermentation, which is shown by its swelling and rising; this, if the ferment was well formed, will be at its height in an hour—somewhat less in very warm weather. It ought to be taken at its height, before it begins to fall.*

Divide the dough into seven equal portions; mould on your paste-board, and form them into loaves; put these on well-floured tin or earthen plates, and place immediately in the oven.

The oven, if a good one, and you have good dry wood, will heat sufficiently in an hour. It is best to kindle the fire in it with dry pine, hemlock furze or some quick burning material; then fill it up with faggots or hard wood split fine and dried, sufficient to heat it—let the wood burn down, and stir the coals evenly over the bottom of the oven, let them lie till they are like embers; the bricks at the arch and sides will be clear from any color of smoke when the oven is sufficiently hot. Clean and sweep the oven,—throw in a little flour on the bottom; if it burns black at once, do not put in the bread, but let it stand a few moments and cool.

It is a good rule to put the fire in the oven when the dough is made up—the latter will rise and the former heat in about the same time.

When the loaves are in the oven, it must be closed and kept tight, except you open it for a moment to see how the bread appears. If the oven is properly heated, loaves of the size named, will be done in an hour and a half or two hours. They will weigh four pounds per loaf, or about that—thus giving you twenty-eight pounds of bread from twenty-one quarts (or pounds) of flour. The weight gained is from the water.

It is the best economy to calculate (or ascertain by experiment) the number of loaves of a certain weight or size, necessary for a week's consumption in your family, and bake accordingly. In the winter season, bread may be kept good for a fortnight; still I think it the best rule to

---

* There are three processes in fermentation—the *vinous*, which makes the dough light and white—the *acetous*, which turns it sour and rather brown—and the *putrefactive*, which utterly spoils it. The only *good bread* is made by baking the dough when the *vinous* fermentation is exactly at its height. As soon as the acetous commences, the dough is injured. It may be in a measure restored by mixing diluted pearlash or sal æratus, and working it thoroughly with every portion of the dough—then baking it quickly.

bake once every week. Bread should not be eaten at all till it has been baked at least one day. When the loaves are done, take them from the oven, and place them on a clean shelf, in a clean, cool pantry. If the crust happen to be scorched, or the bread is too much baked, the loaves, when they are taken out of the oven, may be wrapped in a clean coarse towel, which has been slightly damped. It is well to keep a light cloth thrown over all the loaves. When a loaf has been cut, it should be kept in a tight box from the air, if you wish to prevent its drying.

BROWN OR DYSPEPSIA BREAD.—This bread is now best known as "Graham bread"—not that Doctor Graham invented or discovered the manner of its preparation, but that he has been unwearied and successful in recommending it to the public. It is an excellent article of diet for the dyspeptic and the costive, and, for most persons of sedentary habits, would be beneficial. It agrees well with children; and, in short, I think it should be used in every family, though not to the exclusion of fine bread. The most difficult point in manufacturing this bread, is to obtain good pure meal. It is said that much of the bread commonly sold as *dyspepsia,* is made of the *bran* or *middlings,* from which the fine flour has been separated; and that *saw-dust* is sometimes mixed with the meal. To be certain that it is good, send good, clean wheat to the mill, have it ground rather coarsely, and keep the meal in a dry, cool place. Before using it, sift it through a common hair sieve; this will separate the very coarse and harsh particles.

Take six quarts of this wheat meal, one tea-cup of good yeast, and half a tea-cup of molasses, mix these with a pint of milk-warm water and a tea-spoonful of pearlash or sal æratus. Make a hole in the flour, and stir this mixture in the middle of the meal till it is like batter. Then proceed as with fine flour bread. Make the dough when sufficiently light into four loaves, which will weigh two pounds per loaf when baked. It requires a hotter oven than fine flour bread, and must bake about an hour and a half.

RYE AND INDIAN BREAD.—This is a sweet and nourishing diet, and generally acceptable to children.

It is economical, and when wheat is scarce, is a pretty good substitute for dyspepsia bread.

There are many different proportions of mixing it—some put one third Indian meal with two of rye ; others like one third rye and two of Indian ; others prefer it half and half.

If you use the largest proportion of rye meal, make your dough stiff, so that it will mould into loaves ; when it is two thirds Indian, it should be softer and baked in deep earthen or tin pans, after the following rule :—

Take *four quarts* of sifted Indian meal ; put it into a glazed earthen pan, sprinkle over it a table-spoonful of fine salt ; pour over it about two quarts of boiling water, stir and work it till every part of the meal is thoroughly wet ; Indian meal absorbs a greater quantity of water. When it is about milk-warm, work in *two quarts of rye meal, and half a pint* of lively yeast, mixed with a pint of warm water ; add more warm water, if needed. Work the mixture well with your hands : it should be stiff, but not firm as flour dough. Have ready a large, deep, well-buttered pan ; put in the dough, and smooth the top by putting your hand in warm water, and then patting down the loaf. Set this to rise in a warm place in the winter ; in the summer it should not be put by the fire. When it begins to crack on the top, which will usually be in about an hour or an hour and a half, put it into a well-heated oven, and bake it three or four hours. It is better to let it stand in the oven all night, unless the weather is warm. Indian meal requires to be well cooked. The loaf will weigh between seven and eight pounds. Pan bread keeps best in large loaves.

Many use milk in mixing bread ;—in the country where milk is plentiful, it is a good practice, as bread is certainly richer, wet with sweet milk than with water ; but it will not keep so long in warm weather.

Baking can very well be done in a stove ; during the winter this is an economical way of cooking ; but the stove must be carefully watched, or there is danger of scorching the bread.

RICE BREAD.—Boil a *pint* of *rice* very soft ; when it is nearly cool, add a pint of leaven and work in three quarts of flour. Let it rise, till it is light—one hour, in warm weather, is sufficient; divide the dough into three parts, bake it in tin pans, well buttered; and you will have three large loaves of bread. It soon grows dry.

YEAST.

It is impossible to have good light bread, unless you have lively, sweet *yeast.* When common family beer is well brewed and kept in a clean cask, the settlings are the best of yeast. If you do not keep beer, then make common yeast by the following method :—

Take two quarts of water, one handful of hops, two of wheat bran; boil these together twenty minutes; strain off the water, and while it is boiling hot, stir in either wheat or rye flour, till it becomes a thick batter; let it stand till it is about blood warm; then add a half pint of good smart yeast and a large spoonful of molasses, if you have it, and stir the whole well. Set it in a cool place in summer, and a warm one in winter. When it becomes perfectly light, it is fit for use. If not needed immediately, it should, when it becomes cold, be put in a clean jug or bottle; do not fill the vessel, and the cork must be left loose till the next morning, when the yeast will have done working. Then cork it tightly, and set in a cool place in the cellar. It will keep ten or twelve days.

MILK YEAST.—Take one pint of new milk; one tea-spoonful of fine salt, and a large spoon of flour—stir these well together; set the mixture by the fire, and keep it just lukewarm; it will be fit for use in an hour. Twice the quantity of common yeast is necessary; it will not keep long. Bread made of this yeast dries very soon; but in the summer it is sometimes convenient to make this kind when yeast is needed suddenly.

Never keep yeast in a tin vessel. If you find the old yeast *sour*, and have not time to prepare new, put in sal æratus, a tea-spoonful to a pint of yeast, when ready to use it. If it foams up lively, it will raise the bread; if it does not, never use it.

HARD YEAST.—Boil three ounces of hops in six quarts of water, till only two quarts remain. Strain it, and stir in while it is boiling hot, wheat or rye meal till it is thick as batter. When it is about milk-warm, add half a pint of good yeast, and let it stand till it is very light, which will probably be about three hours. Then work in sifted Indian meal till it is stiff dough. Roll it out on a board; cut it in oblong cakes about three inches by two. They should be about half an inch thick. Lay these cakes on a smooth board, over which a little flour has been dusted; prick them with a fork, and set the board in a dry clean chamber or store-room, where the sun and air may be freely admitted. Turn them every day. They will dry in a fortnight, unless the weather is damp. When the cakes are fully dry, put them into a coarse cotton bag; hang it up in a cool, dry place. If rightly prepared these cakes will keep a year, and save the trouble of making new yeast every week.

Two cakes will make yeast sufficient for a peck of flour. Break them into a pint of lukewarm water, and stir in a large spoonful of flour, the evening before you bake. Set the mixture where it can be kept moderately warm. In the morning it will be fit for use.

ADVANTAGES OF BREAD-MAKING.

If you wish to economize in family expenses, bake your own bread. If this is *good*, it will be better as well as healthier than baker's bread. If you use a stove, you can bake during the winter with very little expense of fuel; and the flour to make bread for a family will cost about one third less than the bread. I knew a family of six persons, who saved fifty dollars by baking their bread during about six months in the year. When flour is cheapest, the saving is greatest.

The rich will find several advantages in having a portion, at least, of their bread baked at home, even though the saving of money should not be an object. They can be *certain* that their bread is made of good flour. This is not always sure when eating baker's bread. Much damaged flour, sour, musty, or grown,* is often used by the public

---

* When the harvest season is very wet, and the wheat cannot be gathered and dried when it is ripe, it often swells in the ear; and this is called *grown grain*. It is very difficult to make light bread from the flour of such grain.

bakers, particularly in scarce or bad seasons. The skill of the baker, and the use of certain ingredients—(alum, ammonia, sulphate of zinc, and even sulphate of copper, it is said, have been used!)—will make this flour into light, white bread. But it is nearly tasteless, and cannot be as healthy or nutritious as bread made from the flour of good, sound wheat, baked at home, without any mixture of drugs and correctives. Even the best of baker's bread is comparatively tasteless, and must be eaten when new to be relished. But good home-baked bread will keep a week, and is better on that account for the health.

Those who live in the country bake their own bread, of course ; and there every lady, old and young, must be, more or less, familiar with the process. But in our cities, ladies marry and commence house-keeping, without knowing any thing of bread-making. Yet there is not one individual, not even the wealthiest, but is liable to be placed in circumstances where the comfort and health of her husband and children may depend, in a great measure, on her own knowledge of this important culinary art.

She may be settled where it is impossible to obtain help, or such as understand their duties ; her skill and judgment, if not her hands, must supply the deficiency. If she cannot do this, she will, if she be a sensible and conscientious woman, feel, with Miss Sedgwick's heroine, in "Means and Ends," that Italian and music are worthless accomplishments compared with the knowledge of bread-making.

Indeed, this knowledge ought to be considered an accomplishment, and, like cake-making, the province of the mistress of the house and her daughters. *Then* the hard, heavy, sour, crude stuff, now often found under the name of "family bread," would not be tolerated. Ladies would be as particular in this respect as in the quality of their cakes. Is it not a thousand times more important that the bread necessary to the health and comfort of those we love, and which is required at every meal, should be made in the best manner, (remember it is a saving of expense to make bread well,) than that the cake made for "the dear five hundred friends," who attend a fashionable party for their own amusement, sometimes found in ridiculing the hostess, should be "superb ?"

It would not require a very great sacrifice of time to attend, once each week, to this department of " household good." If the *sponge* be set at seven or half past, in the morning, and every thing well managed, the bread will be ready to be drawn from the oven by twelve. Four or five hours of attention, then, is required; but three fourths of this time might be employed in needlework, or other pursuits. Only half or three quarters of an hour, devoted to kneading the bread, is wanted in active exertion; and this would be one of the most beneficial exercises our young ladies could practise.

The exercise of the hands and arms, in such a way as to strengthen all the muscles of the body, is very seldom practised by ladies; and hence much of the debility and languor they undergo. Many kinds of household labor are unpleasant, because they soil the clothes, or render the hands dark, rough, and hard. But bread-making (not the heating and cleaning of the oven) is as neat as cake-making; and kneading the dough will make the fairest hand fairer and softer, the exercise giving that healthy pink glow to the palm and nails which is so beautiful.

I have dwelt at length on this subject, because I consider it as important as did " Uncle John," that " Girls should learn to make bread—the staff of life;" and that to do this well is an accomplishment which the lovely and talented should consider indispensable, one of the " *must haves*" of female education.

There are three things which must be exactly *right*, in order to have good bread—the quality of the yeast; the lightness or fermentation of the dough; and the heat of the oven. No precise rules can be given to ascertain these points. It requires observation, reflection, and a quick, nice judgment, to decide when all are right. Thus, you see that bread-making is not a mere mechanical tread-mill operation, like many household concerns, but a work of mind; the woman who always has good home-baked bread on the table shows herself to have good sense and good management.

CHAPTER III.

MEATS.

Effect of animal food—Proper manner of using it—Different kinds of meat—Comparative economy of different modes of cooking—Beef—Pork—Mutton—Lamb—Veal—Venison—Fowls—Birds—Preserving meats.

PHYSICAL health, vigor of mind, and comfort of bodily feeling, depend, in a very great degree, on the manner in which animal food is used. To secure the greatest amount of benefit from this costly* article of diet, which God has appointed for the sustenance, in part, of his rational creatures, three conditions seem indispensable—it must be prepared in a proper way; taken at proper times; and in proper quantities.

The proper manner of preparation is, to cook it till it is entirely *separated from the blood,* and the fibres are rendered soft and easy of digestion.

The proper times of taking meat may be best told by negatives—it is not proper to give it to infants under three years of age; nor should it then be freely given. After the infantile diseases are mostly over, and exercise in the open air is daily practised, the child may be permitted to eat a portion of animal food with its dinner; but not till youth enters on the real labors of life, study, business or work, in good earnest, should a full portion be allowed.

Animal food should never be given to the sick, when any symptoms of excited action in the system from fever are apparent. It should not be taken in large meals by the sedentary, the idle, or the delicate; nor by any person immediately before retiring to rest at night.

There is much more danger of excess in using animal than vegetable food. The reason is that meats can be cooked in a greater variety of ways, are more condensed by cooking, and made so "savory" by seasoning, &c. that

* The cost of *life.*

the taste is tempted when the appetite is satisfied. Not so with plain bread; let it be made in the best possible manner, still we seem to decide, as if by instinct, the exact point when we have had enough.

But meats tax the reasoning powers, observation and reflection, to decide when the proper quantity has been taken. And to understand rightly the nature and regulate the condition of using animal food is an intellectual process, of a much higher kind than is required for the arrangement of a vegetable diet. It is rational then to suppose that animal food strengthens the reasoning powers, or the brain, the organ of the mind, better than vegetable food could do.*

Let no one suppose from this, that the more meat he eats the wiser he will grow. It is using animal food *rightly,* not in gross quantities, which shows that our reason is strengthening. Remember, too, that

" Good things spoiled corrupt to worst."

Oxygen is necessary to support life; but we could not live in an atmosphere of oxygen. The Creator has himself mingled the right proportion of the different gases, which form vital air for the lungs. He has left to our discretion the preparation of food for the stomach, only designating the several kinds of aliment. It would be about as rational to covet pure oxygen to breathe, as to argue that living wholly on animal food would be best, because a portion of it is advantageous.

The quantity of animal food required to sustain the constitution, in its most perfect state, is greatest in the coldest countries, and, decreasing according to the warmth of the climate, when we reach the torrid zone, but a small quantity is needed. In temperate climates, like our own, the largest quantity is required during the winter. None should use it freely during the hottest weather, except it be

---

* The late Doctor Lee, who was principal of the M'Lean Asylum for the Insane, informed me that when patients were brought to him in a raving state, and he found, as was usually the case, that they had been confined to a low, vegetable diet, his first measure was to order for them a good meal of solid food. In almost every instance it proved beneficial in calming the mind. Doctor Lee observed that he considered a portion of animal food indispensable for his patients.

those who labor hard in the open air; it rarely appears to injure such, yet probably it would be best for them to eat less meat and more bread and vegetables during summer. They would not then suffer so much from thirst, which often induces the desire for stimulating liquids.

As a general rule, animal food is more easily and speedily digested than vegetable food of any kind—and this it is which makes meats more heating and stimulating. The great essentials for the easy digestion of animal food are that the fibres be tender and fine grained.

Of the different sorts of butcher meat, *Pork* is that of which the least quantity should be taken at a time. It requires longer to digest roasted pork than any other kind of meat.

Beef agrees well with most constitutions; it is cheapest in the autumn, but best in the winter season. Many have a distaste to mutton; but for those who relish it, it is a nutritious food, and easy of digestion.

Lamb, veal, and fowls are delicate and healthy diet for the young and sedentary; and for all who find fat meats and those of coarse fibre do not agree with them.

The most economical way of cooking meat is to *boil* it, if the liquid be used for soup or broth, as it always ought to be.

Baking is one of the cheapest ways of dressing a dinner in small families, and several kinds of meat are excellent done in this way. Legs and loins of pork, legs of mutton, and fillets of veal will bake to much advantage; especially if they be fat. Never bake a lean, thin piece, it will all shrivel away. Such pieces should always be boiled or made into soup.—Pigs, geese, and the buttock of beef are all excellent baked. Meat always loses in weight by being cooked.—In roasting the loss is the greatest. It also costs more in fuel to roast than to boil—still there are many pieces of meat which seem made for roasting; and it would be almost wrong to cook them in any other way. Those who cannot afford to roast their meat, should not purchase the sirloin of beef.

BEEF.

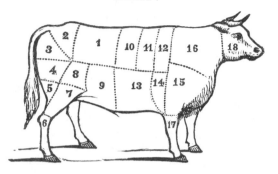

1. Sirloin.—2 Rump.—3. Edge Bone.—4. Buttock.—5. Mouse Buttock.—6. Leg.
—7. Thick Flank.—8. Veiny Piece.—9. Thin Flank.—10. Fore Rib.—11. Middle
Rib.—12. Chuck Rib.—13. Brisket.—14. Shoulder or leg of Mutton Piece.—15.
Clod.—16. Neck, or Sticking Piece.—17. Shin.—18. Cheek.

DIRECTIONS FOR CHOOSING AND COOKING.

Ox beef is considered the best; heifer beef is excellent where well fed, and is most suitable for small families. If you want the best, choose that which has a fine smooth grain—the lean of a bright red; the fat white or nearly so.

The best roasting piece is the sirloin; then the first three ribs—if kept till they are quite tender, and boned, they are nearly equal to the sirloin, and better for a family dinner.

The round is used for *alamode* beef, and is the best piece for corning.

The best beef steak is cut from the inner part of the sirloin. Good steak may be cut from the ribs.

If you wish to practise economy, buy the chuck, or piece between the shoulder and the neck; it makes a good roast or steak, and is excellent for stewing or baking. The thick part of the flank is also a profitable piece; good to bake or boil, or even roast.

The leg and shin of beef make the best soup—the heart is profitable meat, and good broiled or roasted. The leg rand is used for mince pies—it needs to be boiled till it is very tender. The tongue, when fresh, is a rich part for mince pies. If eaten by itself, it should be pickled and smoked.

The other pieces of the animal are best salted and boiled; or if used fresh, stewed or in soups. Beef should rarely be fried.

Fresh beef is better for being kept three or four days in moderate, and much longer in cold weather. One reason why beef is not so good or wholesome in summer is, that it must be eaten too fresh, and while the fibre is tough, or it will spoil. Do not attempt to keep it longer than till the second day in hot weather. In the winter, if frozen, and packed in snow, it may be kept many days, even weeks. To thaw frozen meat, always lay it in cold water; and allow one third longer time to cook meat in the winter, especially if it has been frozen, than would be required in warm weather.

When beef is to be kept for any length of time, it should be carefully wiped every day. In warm weather, it is well to sprinkle it over with pepper to keep it from the flies. Should it become in the least tainted, wash it in cold water, then in strong camomile tea, afterwards sprinkle it with salt, if it is not to be used till the following day. It must be again thoroughly washed in cold water, before it is cooked. Roughly-pounded charcoal rubbed all over the meat will remove the taint.

These directions equally apply to all sorts of meat.

To ROAST BEEF.—The sirloin is too large for a private family; one weighing fifteen pounds is the best size for roasting; but this may be divided if a small one is required. It should be washed in cold water, then dried with a clean cloth and rubbed over with salt, and the fat covered with a piece of white paper tied on with thread. The spit should be clean as sand and water can make it. Be sure and wipe it dry immediately after it is drawn from the meat, and scour and wash it always before using.

The fire must be bright and clear, but not scorching, when the meat is put down. Place it about ten inches from the fire at first, and gradually move it nearer. It should be basted with a little clean dripping or lard, put into the roaster or tin-kitchen, as soon as it is down. Be sure this roaster is perfectly clean. Continue to baste the meat at intervals and turn the spit frequently, and when the roast is nearly done, or about half an hour before you take it up —remove the paper from the fat, sprinkle on a little salt, and baste it well—pour off the top of the dripping, which is nearly all liquid fat, and would prove unhealthy if used in the gravy; then take a tee-cup of boiling water, into which put a salt-spoonful of salt, and drop this, by degrees, on the brown parts of the joint, (the meat will soon brown again.) —Stir the fire and make it clear; sprinkle a little salt over the roast, baste it with butter and dredge it with flour—very soon the froth will rise; then it must be taken up directly and dished.—Pour the gravy from the roaster, skim it, and give it a boil, then send it to table in a boat. Scraped horse-radish is used to garnish the roast, or may be sent up in a plate with vinegar.

The inside of the sirloin is excellent for hash.

Twenty minutes of time to each pound of meat is the rule for roasting. In cold weather, and when the meat is very fat, it will require a little more time. In warm weather, and with lean beef, fifteen minutes to a pound will be sufficient. Experience and judgment must regulate these things.

Beef alamode.—Take a thick piece of beef, six pounds, bone it, beat it well, then put it into a stewpan with some rind of bacon, an onion, a bunch of sweet herbs, some cloves, salt, and pepper, pour over the whole a quart of water, let it stew over a slow fire for four hours at least. A clean cloth should be placed over the stewpan before the lid is put on, which must be carefully closed. When it is done, strain the gravy through a sieve, clear off the fat, and serve.

Beef baked.—Let a buttock of beef, weighing ten pounds, which has been in salt about three days, be well washed and put into an earthen pan, with a pint of water; season with pepper, cloves, and a minced onion; cover the pan tight with two or three sheets of paper—let it bake four or five hours in a moderately heated oven.

Beef baked with Potatoes.—Boil some potatoes, peel, and pound them in a mortar with one or two small onions; moisten them with milk and an egg beaten up; add a little salt and pepper. Season slices of beef, or mutton chops, with salt and pepper, rub the bottom of a pudding-dish with butter, and put a layer of the mashed potatoes, which should be as thick as batter, and then a layer of meat, and so on alternately till the dish is filled, ending with potatoes. Bake it in an oven for one hour.

BEEF STEWED.—Take ten pounds of a brisket of beef, cut the short ribs, and put it into a saucepan, with two large onions, stuck with three or four cloves, two or three carrots cut into quarters, a bunch of sweet herbs, a small lemon sliced, and five quarts of water; skim it well; let it stew seven hours. Strain and clarify the gravy—thicken it with butter and flour. Chop the carrots with some capers, mushroom catsup, or Cayenne. Any other pickle that is liked may be added.

To PRESS BEEF.—Take the bones from the brisket or flank, or the thin part of the ribs. Salt, and season it well with mixed spices, adding sugar also, and let it lie a week, rubbing it every day with the pickle; then stew it in just sufficient water to cover it, till tender, when it must be rolled tightly in a cloth, and pressed with a heavy weight till cold.

A *Porker's* or *Calf's Head* may be pressed in the same way. The porker's head should be salted before boiling. The calf's head is boiled fresh, then seasoned as for hash, and pressed.

BEEF BOILED.—The perfection of boiling is that it be done slowly and the pot well skimmed. If the scum be permitted to boil down, it sticks to the meat and gives it a dirty appearance. A quart of water to a pound of meat is an old rule; but there must always be water sufficient to cover it well, so that the scum may be taken off easily.

When beef is very salt (which it rarely will be if rightly cured) it must be soaked for half an hour or more in lukewarm water, before it is put on to boil, when the water must be changed.

The ROUND is the best piece to boil—then the H-BONE. Take part of a ROUND of beef—put into your boiler with plenty of cold water to cover it; set the pot on one side of the fire to boil gently ; if it boil *quick* at first, no art can make the meat tender. *The slower it boils the tenderer it will be.*

(How much good fuel is wasted, to say nothing of the hard labor cooks impose on themselves and the injury to their health by heating over a great blaze, through this carelessness in making fires! In the country, especially, and often during summer, a fire is prepared nearly hot enough for Nebuchadnezzar's furnace, merely to boil the pot! Instead of hanging the boiler low, it seems the ambition of the housewife to elevate it as near the stars as possible. Three small sticks of wood, or two with chips, will boil a large dinner, and if the pot is hung very low, but little inconvenience will be felt from the fire. This in hot weather, for those who are obliged to be in the kitchen, is a great comfort. But the pot is boiling all this time—so to our receipt.)

Be sure to take off all the scum as it rises. When you take the meat up, if any stray scum sticks to it, wash it off with a paste brush. Garnish the dish with carrots and turnips. Boiled potatoes, carrots, turnips and greens, on separate plates, are good accompaniments.

If the beef weigh ten pounds it requires to boil, or rather simmer, about three hours. In cold weather all meats need to be cooked a longer time than in warm weather. Always cook them till tender.

BEEF STEAKS BROILED.—The inside of the sirloin is the best steak—but all are cooked in the same manner. Cut them about three quarters of an inch thick—do not beat them ; it breaks the cells in which the gravy of the meat is contained, and renders it drier and more tasteless.

Have the gridiron hot and the bars rubbed with suet— the fire clear and brisk ; sprinkle a little salt over the fire, lay on the steaks, and turn them often. Keep a dish close to the fire, into which you must drain the gravy from the top of the steak as you lift it to turn. The gridiron should be set in a slanting direction on the coals, to prevent the fat from dropping into the fire and making a smoke. But should a smoke occur, take off the gridiron a moment, till it is over. With a good fire of coals, steaks will be thoroughly done in twelve or fifteen minutes. These are much healthier for delicate stomachs than *rare-done steaks.*

When done, lay them in a hot plate, put a small slice of good butter on each piece—sprinkle a *little* salt, pour the gravy from the dish by the fire, and serve them hot as possible. Pickles and finely-scraped horse-radish are served with them.

I have now given the most important receipts for cooking beef.—The re-cooking requires skill and judgment, which experience only can give. When well done, it makes excellent dishes, and is economical in house-keeping. The following are good receipts :—

BEEF, COLD TENDERLOIN.—Cut off entire the inside of a large sirloin of beef, brown it all over in a stewpan, and then add a quart of water, two table spoonfuls of vinegar, some pepper, salt, and a large onion finely minced; cover the pan closely, and let it stew till the beef is very tender. Garnish with pickles.

BEEF, COLD STEAKS TO WARM.—Lay them in a stewpan, with one large onion cut in quarters, six berries of allspice, the same of black pepper, cover the steaks with boiling water, let them stew gently one hour, thicken the liquor with flour and butter rubbed together on a plate; if a pint of gravy, about one spoonful of flour, and the like of butter, will do; put it into the stewpan, shake it well over the fire for five minutes, and it is ready; lay the steaks and onions on a dish, and pour the gravy through a sieve over them.

BEEF MINCED.—Mince your beef very small; put it into a saucepan with a little gravy and a little of the fat of fowl or any other fat, season according to your taste, then let it simmer over a gentle fire; but do not let it boil.

Boiled beef, when thoroughly done, is excellent to eat cold, as a relish for breakfast. The slices should be cut even and very thin.

PORK.

1. Leg.—2. Hind Loin.—3. Fore Loin.—4. Spare Rib.—5. Hand.—6. Belly, or Spring.

Pork that is fed from the dairy, and fattened on corn, is the best—potatoes do very well for part of the feeding. But pork fattened from the still-house is all but poisonous; it should never be eaten by Christians or those who wish to preserve their health.

The offals, &c., with which pork in the vicinity of a city is fattened, make it unsavory and unwholesome. Such stuff should be used for manure, and never given as food to animals whose flesh is to be eaten by man.

When pork is good, the flesh looks very white and smooth, and the fat white and fine. Hogs two years old make the best—older than that, their flesh is apt to be rank. Measly pork is very unwholesome, and never should be eaten. It may be known, as the fat is filled with small kernels.

When the rind is thick and tough, and cannot easily be impressed with the finger, the pork is old, and will require more cooking.

If pork is not cooked enough, it is disagreeable and almost indigestible; it should never be eaten unless it is thoroughly done.

The fat parts of pork are not very healthy food. Those who labor hard may feel no inconvenience from this diet; but children should never eat it; nor is it healthy for the delicate and sedentary. Fat pork seems more proper as material for frying fish and other meats, and as a garnish, than to be cooked and eaten by itself. It is best and least apt to prove injurious during the cold weather.

The lean, especially the ham, is excellent; and when

eaten moderately, seldom proves injurious; but a full meal of roast pork or pig is a hazardous experiment. Unless the stomach be very strong, it will cause heaviness and nausea.

In short, there is no doubt that pork is the kind of meat which should be most sparingly used in substance. As an auxiliary in the culinary department, we could not comfortably dispense with it.

To ROAST.—Take a leg of pork, one weighing eight pounds will require full three and a half hours to roast it. Wash it clean, but do not *soak* it, and dry it with a cloth; with a sharp knife score the skin in diamonds about an inch square.

Make a stuffing with grated bread, a little sage, and two small onions chopped fine, seasoned with pepper and salt, and moistened with the yolk of an egg. Put this in under the skin of the knuckle, and in deep incisions made in the thick part of the leg; rub a little fine-powdered sage into the skin where it is scored; and then, with a paste brush or goose feather, rub the whole surface of the skin with sweet oil or butter. This makes the crackling crisper and browner than basting it with dripping; it will be perfect in color, and the skin will not blister.

Do not put it too near the fire; and it must be moistened at intervals with sweet oil or butter, tied up in a rag. When it is done, skim the fat from the gravy, which may be thickened with a little butter rolled in flour.

Apple-sauce is always proper to accompany roasted pork —this, with potatoes, mashed or plain, mashed turnips, and pickles, is good.

SPARE-RIB—should be rubbed with powdered sage mixed with salt and pepper, before it is roasted. It will require, if large and thick, two or three hours to roast it—a very thin one may roast in an hour. Lay the thick end to the fire. When you put it down, dust on some flour, and baste with a little butter.

The shoulder, loin, or chine are roasted in the same manner. A shoulder is the most economical part to buy, and is excellent boiled. Pork is always salted before it is boiled.

PICKLED PORK takes more time than other meat. If you buy your pork ready salted, ask how many days it has been in salt; if many, it will require to be soaked in water before you dress it. When you cook it, wash and scrape it as clean as possible; when delicately dressed, it is a favorite dish with almost every body. Take care it does not boil fast; if it does, the knuckle will break to pieces, before the thick part of the meat is warm through; a leg of seven pounds takes three hours and a half very slow simmering. Skim your pot very carefully, and when you take the meat out of the boiler, scrape it clean.

The proper vegetables are parsnips, potatoes, turnips, or carrots. Some like cabbage; but it is a strong, rank vegetable, and does not agree with a delicate stomach. It should not be given to children.

PORK STEAKS.—Cut them off a neck or loin; trim them neatly, and pepper them; broil them over a clear fire, turning them frequently; they will take twenty minutes. Sprinkle with salt when put in the plate, and add a small piece of butter.

BROILED HAM.—Cut ham into very thin slices, and broil on a gridiron. If the ham is too salt, soak the slices before broiling, in cold water; if you are obliged to do this, dry them well with a cloth before broiling.

Fry what eggs you want in butter, and when dished lay an egg on each slice of ham, and serve.

HAM BOILED.—A ham, if dry, requires to be soaked from twelve to twenty-four hours in warm water. Then put it on in cold water, and let it simmer, not boil, four or five hours. When done, pull off the skin neatly, and keep it to cover the ham when set by, cold; strew bread crumbs over it, and place it on a hot dish set over the pot before the fire to crisp; or put it in the oven. It is better and goes further not to be cut till it is quite cold. Boiled ham is delicate to broil.

SAUSAGES FRIED.—Sausages are best when quite fresh. Put a little dripping or bit of butter in the frying pan; as soon as it is melted, put in the sausages and shake them and turn often. Fry them over a very slow fire, and be sure not to break or prick them. Fry them till they are a nice brown—then drain them from the fat, and serve.

They are easily digested, and a very nutritious food—proper for the elderly whose teeth are not good.

To make Sausage Meat.—Chop two pounds of lean with one of fat pork very fine—mix with this meat five tea-spoonfuls of salt, seven of powdered sage, two of black pepper, and one of cloves. You can add a little rosemary, if you like it.

To roast a Pig.—A pig about three weeks old is the best. It should be killed in the morning, if it is to be eaten for dinner.

Make the stuffing with about six ounces of grated bread, a handful of sage minced fine, (or two ounces,) and a large onion. Mix these together with an egg, some pepper, salt, and a bit of butter as large as an egg.

Wash the pig in cold water, cut off the pettitoes, leaving the skin long to wrap around the ends of the legs. Then fill the belly with the stuffing, and sew it up. The liver and heart may be kept with the feet for gravy.

The fire must be clear and hotter at the ends than in the middle. You can place a flat-iron before the middle of the fire.

Before the pig is put down, rub it over with salad oil or fresh butter, and baste with these till it is done. It requires constant care. A small one will be done enough in an hour and a half.

Before you take it from the fire, cut off the head and part it down the middle, take out the brains, chop them fine with some boiled sage-leaves, and mix these with veal or beef gravy, or that which runs from the pig when you cut it down the middle, which must be done before you lay it in the dish.

MUTTON.

Mutton is best from August till January. It is nutritious, and often agrees better than any other meat with weak stomachs. To have it tender, it must be kept as long as possible without injury. Be sure and cook it till it is *done*; the gravy that runs when the meat is cut should *never show he least tinge of blood.* It is an abomination to serve it as some do, half raw.

To roast mutton, make a brisk fire, and allow fifteen or twenty minutes to the pound. Paper the fat parts. Baste and froth it the same as beef.

The hind quarter or haunch is the prime piece to roast— the leg, loin, neck and breast may all be cooked in this manner—though it is more profitable to boil the leg. The following is a good receipt :—

A STUFFED LOIN OF MUTTON.—Take the skin off a loin of mutton with the flap on; bone it neatly; make a nice veal stuffing,* and fill the inside of the loin with it where the bones were removed; roll it up tight, skewer the flap, and tie twine round it to keep it firmly together; put the outside skin over it till nearly roasted, and then remove it that the mutton may brown. Serve with a nice gravy, mash-ed turnips and potatoes. Currant jelly is eaten with mutton.

Mutton must be boiled the same as other meats—that is, *simmered very slowly*, and the scum carefully removed. Always wash it before cooking, and put it in cold water. Only allow water sufficient to cover it, and the liquor makes excellent broth, with a little rice and a few carrots, &c.

Mutton for boiling must not be kept so long as it may be for roasting. Two or three days is sufficient; in warm weather less.

MUTTON LEG TO BOIL.—Cut off the shank bone, and trim the knuckle—if it weigh nine pounds it will require three hours to cook it.

Parsley and butter, or caper-sauce, should be served with it—onion sauce, turnips, spinach, and potatoes are all used.

To STEW A SHOULDER OF MUTTON.—Bone and flatten a shoulder of mutton, sprinkle over it pepper and salt, roll it up tightly, bind it with tape, and put it into a stewpan that will just hold it, pour over it a well-seasoned gravy made with the bones, cover the pan closely, and let it stew till

---

* *A good Stuffing for Veal, Mutton, or Poultry.*—Take two cups of bread crumbs and one of butter or minced suet, a little parsley finely shred, the quarter of a nutmeg grated, a tea-spoonful of powdered lemon peel, allspice and salt—the whole to be worked together with two or three yolks of egg, well beat.

tender; before serving, take off the tape, and thicken the gravy. It will take about three hours to stew the shoulder.

Mutton Chops.—Cut the chops off a loin or the best end of a neck of mutton; pare off the fat, dip them in a beaten egg and strew over them grated bread, seasoned with salt and finely-minced parsley; then fry them in a little butter, and make a gravy, or broil them over coals, and butter them in a hot dish. Garnish with fried parsley.

LAMB.

1. Leg.—2. Shoulder.—3. Loin, Best End.—4. Loin, Chump End.—5. Neck, Best End.—6. Breast.—7. Neck, Scrag End.
Note. A Chine is two Loins: and a Saddle is two Loins, and two Necks of the Best End.

Lamb is a delicate and tender meat; but it requires to be kept a few days, when the weather will permit—and should be thoroughly cooked to be healthful. Never take lamb or veal from the spit till the gravy that drops is white.

The fore quarter of lamb consists of the shoulder, neck and breast together; this is best roasted; it requires about two hours to cook it well. The leg may be boiled or roasted.

Lamb is fine for cutlets, or with rice cooked as follows :—

Lamb dressed with Rice.—Half roast a small fore quarter; cut it into steaks; season them with a little salt and pepper; lay them into a dish, and pour in a little water. Boil a pound of rice with a blade or two of mace; strain it, and stir in a good piece of fresh butter, and a little salt, add also the greater part of the yolk of four eggs beaten; cover the lamb with the rice, and with a feather put over it the remainder of the beaten eggs. Bake it in an oven till it has acquired a light brown color.

VEAL.

1. Loin, Best End.—2. Fillet.—3. Loin, Chump End.—4. Hind Knuckle.—5. Neck, Best End.—6. Breast, Be t End.—7. Blade Bone, or Oyster-part.—8. Fore Knuckle.—9. Breast, Brisket End.—10. Neck, Scrag End.

The *loin* is the best part of a calf, and requires to be roasted about three hours. Paper the kidney—if it be very fat, cut off a part before roasting, it is excellent suet. Both the *fillet* and *shoulder* should be stuffed before roasting. [See *Loin of Mutton.*]

The fillet is good stewed like a shoulder of mutton.

The neck of veal makes fine cutlets—season and fry or broil like mutton chops.

Veal is a delicate meat, but not easy of digestion unless it be done very tender. Broiled, it is most difficult to digest. When boiled, stewed, or made into soup, it must be very carefully skimmed, as it sends up a great quantity of scum, and is easily discolored.

The knuckle is best stewed, as the whimsical receipt of Gay, the poet, testifies :—

> "Take a knuckle of veal,
> (You may buy it or steal,)
> In a few pieces cut it,
> In a stewing-pan put it."

Where it must remain (seasoned with a great variety of sweet herbs) about three hours, when it is fit for any dignitary.

The knuckle is also excellent boiled, if the gristles are made perfectly tender. Serve parsley and melted butter in a boat ; or veal gravy with the parsley is much better.

The liquor of boiled veal should always be saved and boiled down for gravy, if not made into broth.

VENISON.

It hardly seems worth while to give receipts for cooking venison, so little is to be had in the markets. It is said to be the most easily digested of any kind of meat, consequently would be good food for those who are troubled with weak and slow digestive powers, if it could be obtained. It ought to be kept some time—a fortnight, if the weather permit—after it is killed; then roasted before a strong close fire. The fat parts must be covered with paper and a paste made of flour and water to prevent burning—baste it well; a haunch of twelve pounds will require about four hours to roast. Currant jelly is served with it.

VENISON STEAKS—may be broiled or fried in the same manner as mutton chops or veal cutlets. Mutton is the best substitute for the real venison; dressed by the following receipt, it is much relished :—

VENISON MOCK.—Hang up, for several days, a large fat loin of mutton; then bone it, and take off all the kidney-fat, and the skin from the upper fat; mix together one ounce of ground allspice, two ounces of brown sugar and one ounce of ground black pepper. Rub it well into the mutton; keep it covered with the skin; rub and turn it daily for five days. When to be roasted, cover it with the skin, and paper it the same way as venison is done. Serve it with made gravy, and currant jelly. It must be well washed from the spices before it is roasted.

POULTRY.

No kind of animal food is so delicate and delicious as the flesh of fowls and birds, and no kind is so generally healthful. Rarely does it disagree with those who are well; even the feeble in constitution, or those debilitated by sickness, find this a most agreeable and nutritious diet.

The white meat of a young turkey, when well boiled, is easier of digestion than that of any other fowl.

In a young turkey, the toes and bill are soft.

A young goose (a very old one is not fit to be eaten) is

plump in the breast, and the fat white and soft—the feet yellow, the web of the foot thin and tender.

Ducks, if young, feel very tender under the wing, and the web of the foot is transparent.

The best fowls have yellow legs—if very old, the feet look stiff and worn.

Pigeons should be quite fresh, the breast plump and fat.

Poultry should lie one night after being killed in warm weather to make it tender; in cold weather it may be kept a much longer time to advantage.

To prepare fowls for cooking, pick out every pin-feather, take out the gall bag without breaking, singe off the hairs over a quick blaze, made with white paper is the best; wash thoroughly, passing a stream of cold water again and again through the inside; cut off the head, feet and neck; boil the latter with the liver and gizzard (well cleaned) in a small quantity of water for gravy; then,

To ROAST A TURKEY.—Make a stuffing like that for veal; or take a tea-cup of sausage meat and add a like quantity of bread crumbs, with the beaten yolk of two eggs—then fill the crop; dredge the turkey over with flour, lay it before the fire, taking care this is most on the stuffed part, as that requires the greatest heat. A strip of paper may be put on the breast bone to prevent its scorching. Baste with a little butter or salt and water at first, then with its own dripping. A little before it is taken up, dredge it again with flour, baste with butter and froth it up. A larger turkey requires full three hours' roasting—a smaller one in proportion.

Ham or tongue is usually eaten with turkey; stewed cranberries also.

To BOIL A TURKEY.—Clean it as to roast, make a stuffing of bread, green parsley, one lemon peel, a few oysters or an onion—season with salt, pepper, a little nutmeg, and mix one egg and a small bit of butter; put this into the crop, fasten up the skin, put the turkey on in cold water enough to cover it, let it boil slowly, and take off all the scum; when this is done, it should only simmer closely covered till it is done. It will take about two hours for a small turkey, longer if large. A little salt may be put in the water, and the turkey dredged with flour before it is boiled. The neck and liver are boiled, chopped and put in the gravy.

Fowls and *Chickens* may be boiled in the same way, with a like stuffing, only allowing less time. A chicken will take about thirty-five minutes,; a fowl *nearly an hour.* Let them boil till tender—serve with parsley-sauce or egg-sauce.

Fowls and chickens are cooked in a great variety of ways. Fowls are good stuffed and roasted, the same as turkies, only allowing less time at the fire; an hour and a half for a large fowl—not quite an hour for a chicken; this last need not be stuffed.

It is needless to repeat over again the ingredients for stuffing, way of making gravy, &c. A female who has sense enough to cook a dinner will manage these things to her own liking and means. It is not necessary to good cooking, that every one should season alike.

Young chickens are best broiled or fricasseed.

To BROIL A CHICKEN.—Pick and singe them nicely, wash them clean, and dry them in a cloth; cut them down the back, truss the legs and wings, as for boiling; flatten them, and put them upon a cold gridiron over hot coals; when they become a little dry, put them upon a plate, turn them, butter and strew a little salt and pepper over the inside, which part is laid first upon the gridiron: turn them frequently, and let them broil slowly for about half an hour. Serve them hot, with melted butter poured over them, or plenty of stewed mushrooms. The livers and gizzards may be broiled with them, fastened into the wings, well seasoned and served with the chickens.

To FRICASSEE A CHICKEN.—Wash and cut the chicken into joints; scald and take off the skin, put the pieces in a stewpan, with an onion cut small, a bunch of parsley, a little thyme and lemon-peel, salt and pepper—add a pint of water, a bit of butter as large as an egg. Stew it an hour; a little before serving, add the yolks of two eggs beaten up, with a tea-cup of sweet cream, stirring it in gradually; take care that this gravy does not boil.

CHICKEN BAKED IN RICE.—Cut a chicken into joints as for a fricassee, season it well with pepper and salt, lay it into a pudding-dish lined with slices of ham or bacon, add a pint of veal gravy, and an onion finely minced; fill up the dish with boiled rice well pressed and piled as high as the dish will hold, cover it with a paste of flour and water, and bake one hour in a slow oven. If you have no veal gravy, use water instead adding a little more ham and seasoning.

To ROAST A GOOSE.—Geese seem to bear the same relation to poultry that pork does to the flesh of other domestic quadrupeds; that is, the flesh of goose is not suitable for, or agreeable to, the very delicate in constitution. One reason doubtless is, that it is the fashion to bring it to table very rare done; a detestable mode!

Take a young goose, pick, singe, and clean well. Make the stuffing with two ounces of onions, (about four common sized,) and one ounce of green sage chopped very fine; then add a large coffee cup of stale bread crumbs and the same of mashed potatoes; a little pepper and salt, a bit of butter as big as a walnut, the yolk of an egg or two; mix these well together, and stuff the goose; do not fill it entirely—the stuffing requires room to swell. Spit it; tie the spit at both ends, to prevent its swinging round, and to keep the stuffing from coming out. The fire must be brisk. Baste it with salt and water at first—then with its own dripping. It will take two hours or more to roast it thoroughly.

A green goose, that is, one under four months old, is seasoned with pepper and salt, instead of sage and onions. It will roast in an hour.

DUCK, TO ROAST,—may be stuffed the same as a goose. It will roast in an hour, or less if it be young.

DUCK, TO STEW.—Cut one or two ducks into quarters; fry them a light brown in butter; put them into a saucepan, with a pint of gravy, four onions whole, pepper, and some salt, a bunch of parsley, two sage leaves, a sprig of winter savory, and sweet marjoram. Cover the pan closely, and stew them till tender; take out the herbs and pepper; skim it; if the sauce be not sufficiently thick, mix with two table-spoonfuls of it a little flour, and stir it into the sauce-pan; boil it up, and garnish the dish with the four onions.

Both geese and ducks, if old, are better to be parboiled before they are roasted. Put them on in just sufficient water to boil them; keep the vessel close covered; let a tough goose simmer two hours, then dry and wipe it clean; stuff and roast, basting it at first with a little bacon fat or butter.

PIGEONS.—About the only birds in New England worth cooking, are the pigeon and partridge. A few quails and woodcocks are occasionally found; the robin is sometimes killed; but it is a sin against feeling to destroy a singing bird—one, too, so innocent and gentle. Any one who kills a robin to eat, ought to have it hung round his neck as the albatross was around the "Ancient Mariner."

Pigeons are dry and easily-digested food, but not quite so delicate as partridges. For the sick, the latter are very appropriate, and may be eaten, if good, (they are some-times almost poisonous, in the early spring, supposed to be caused by feeding on a certain berry,) when other meats would be injurious.

Pigeons may be broiled like chickens, or roasted, only tying over the breast thin slices of fat bacon. When the bird is nearly done, then remove the bacon; dredge with flour; baste with a little butter and froth. They will roast in about half an hour. They may be stuffed or not, as you like. Make a gravy with the giblets, mixed with parsley, seasoned with pepper and salt, and thickened with a little flour and butter.

To STEW PIGEONS.—Wash and clean six pigeons, cut them into quarters, and put all their giblets with them into a stewpan, a piece of butter, a little water, a bit of lemon-peel, two blades of mace, some chopped parsley, salt, and pepper; cover the pan closely, and stew them till they are tender; thicken the sauce with the yolk of an egg beaten up with three table-spoonfuls of cream and a bit of butter dusted with flour; let them stew ten minutes longer before serving. This is an excellent and economical way of cook-ing them.

Partridges may be roasted like pigeons; but they are better stewed, because such dry meat.

To stew Partridges.—Truss two partridges as fowls are done for boiling ; pound the livers with double the quantity of fat bacon and bread crumbs boiled in milk, add some chopped parsley and mushrooms; season with pepper, salt, grated lemon-peel, and mace.   Stuff the inside of the birds, tie them at both ends, and put them into a stewpan lined with slices of bacon; add a quart of good gravy, if you have it, otherwise water, two onions, a bunch of sweet herbs, and a few blades of mace ; let them stew gently till tender ; take them out, strain and thicken the sauce with flour and butter, make it hot and pour it over the partridges.

PRESERVING MEATS.

Salt is the grand preservative of meats; but in using these, care should be taken to soak them if too salt.   It is not healthy to eat our food very salt.

In the summer season particular attention must be observed, lest fresh meat be injured.   In the country this care is very necessary.

Be sure and take the kernels out of a round of beef; one in the udder, in the fat, and those about the thick end of the flank.

To salt the meat thoroughly, rub in the salt evenly into every part, and fill the holes where the kernels were taken out.

A pound and a half of salt will be sufficient for twenty-five pounds of beef, if you only want to corn it to be eaten in a few days.

In the summer, the sooner meat is salted, after it is cool, the better.   In winter, it is better to be kept a few days before salting.

Pork ought not to be allowed to freeze before it is salted for family use.

If you wish beef to look red, rub it first with saltpetre and sugar ; half an ounce of each mixed together, is sufficient for twenty pounds of meat.

PICKLE FOR BEEF.—Allow to four gallons of water two pounds of brown sugar, six pounds of salt, and four ounces of saltpetre; boil it about twenty minutes, taking off the scum as it rises; the following day pour it over the meat which has been packed into the pickling tub. Pour off this brine, boil and skim it every two months, adding three ounces of brown sugar and half a pound of common salt. By this means it will keep good a year. The meat must be sprinkled with salt, and the next day wiped dry, before pouring the pickle over it, with which it should always be completely covered.

Canvass lids should be placed over salting tubs, to admit air and exclude flies, which are more destructive to salting meat than to fresh.

AN EXCELLENT PICKLE FOR HAMS, TONGUES, &c.— Take one gallon of water, one pound and a half of salt, one pound of brown sugar or molasses, one ounce of allspice, and one ounce of saltpetre; scald, skim, and let it cool. Rub the meat with salt, and let it lie two days; then pour the pickle over it. Let the hams, &c. remain from a fortnight to a month in this pickle, according to their size, turning them every day.

Care must be taken to secure bacon and hams from the fly. The best method is, to put them in coarse calico or canvass bags; paper is apt to break in damp weather. Always keep smoked meat in a dark place.

To SALT FAT PORK.—Pack it down tightly in the barrel, each layer of pork covered with clean coarse salt; then make a strong brine with two gallons of water and as much coarse salt as will dissolve in it; boil and skim; let it stand till it is perfectly cold, and then pour it to the meat till that is covered. Pork is best without sugar or saltpetre, provided it be always kept covered with this strong brine.

An excellent way to keep fresh meat during the winter, is practised by the farmers in the country, which they term "salting in snow." Take a large clean tub, cover the bottom three or four inches thick with clean snow; then lay in pieces of fresh meat, spare-ribs, fowls, or whatever you wish to keep, and cover each layer with two or three

inches of snow, taking particular care to fill snow into
every cranny and crevice between the pieces, and around
the edges of the tub. Fowls must also be filled inside with
the snow. When the tub is filled, the last layer must be
snow, pressed down tight; then cover the tub, which must
be kept in a cold place, the colder the better. The meat
will not freeze, and unless there happen to be a long *spell*
of warm weather, the snow will not thaw, but the meat remain as fresh and juicy when it is taken out to be cooked,
as when it was first killed.

To salt Beef *for immediate use, and to make Soup of.*
—Take the thin flank or brisket; cut it into pieces of the
size you wish for your family—from three to seven pounds.
Rub the pieces thoroughly with dry salt; then lay them in
a tub, and cover it close. Turn the pieces every day, and
in a week it will be excellent boiled with vegetables, or
made into plain pease or potato soup. From that time to
six weeks it will be good for the same purpose. It is better
economy and healthier to prepare beef in this manner, than
to buy it fresh every day.

Mutton may be salted in the same manner.

To smoke Hams and Fish on a small scale.—Drive
the ends out of an old hogshead or barrel. Place this
over a heap of sawdust of green hard wood, in which a
bar of red-hot iron is buried; or take corn-cobs, which
make the best smoke, place them in a clean iron kettle,
the bottom of which is covered with live coals. Hang the
Hams, Tongues, Fish, &c. on sticks across the cask, and
cover it to confine the smoke, giving it a very little air, that
the cobs or sawdust, &c. may smoulder slowly, but not
burn.

In Scotland, dried juniper wood is thought to give a delicious flavor when used in smoking meat.

Always bear in mind that to *eat the blood* of animals is
as positively forbidden by God as to *shed the blood* of a
brother. In this view, the Scotch *black puddings*, made
of *hog's blood!* are an abomination, which it is strange a
Christian can partake.

CHAPTER IV.

SOUPS AND GRAVIES.

Soups hurtful to Dyspeptics—suitable for the Healthy—Economic
way of making Soups and Gravies—Turtle Soup—Currie—Veal
—Beef or Mutton —White — Pigeon —Vegetable—Rice—Peas—
For an Invalid—Gravies—Melted Butter.

ONE of the popular errors in regard to diet is consider-
ing soups and broths as light food, and therefore always
proper for weak stomachs and feeble constitutions.

"O, this nice broth cannot hurt you!" — "The hot
soup must do you good this cold day," is often said to the
poor shivering dyspeptic, or drooping invalid. And if they
take this food and are injured by it—why, their case must
be desperate, indeed, not to bear a little soup!

In Dr. Beaumont's experiments on the effect of the gastric
fluid on the different kinds of food usually taken into the
stomach, soups were found to be among the most indigestible ; and the reason is, that the water in the soup must
be separated from the nourishment before the process of
digestion can begin. This separation takes some time ;
then if the stomach be weak or diseased, and secrete (or
form) but little gastric juice, this becomes diluted and the
action of the stomach materially deranged by the effort of
separating the water from the nutritive particles in the
soup. Dyspeptics, therefore, should not take this kind of
food ; nor any kind that is very liquid. Bilious persons,
and those who are troubled with heart-burn and indigestion,
would be injured by eating soups often. For children, if a
good share of rice and other vegetables be in the liquid, or
considerable bread eaten with it, soup is a generally healthy
and invigorating food ; and for those who are in health
and labor hard, and require large meals, it is a good plan to
begin the dinner with soup of some kind, as otherwise they
would be inclined to take too much solid food.

With these restrictions, then, the good housekeeper will

know how to plan her soup days, and for whom to make this savory dish, one of the most delicious when well prepared.

I have before remarked, that the liquor in which meats of all kinds are boiled, (except smoked meats,) should be saved and used, either in soups or gravies. This liquor contains much of the essence of the meat, (if the pot was kept closely covered, which it always should be when meats are boiling,) and, if rightly prepared, will prove a great saving in the expense for animal food in a family. If the meats or poultry are boiled for the table, it is better not to use the liquor the first day. Pour it into a well-glazed earthen pot or pan, and let it stand till the next morning. Then skim off the fat, and strain the liquid into a clean soup-boiler. By this means you entirely *separate the blood from the meat,* which is the great object of cookery, and should be as conscientiously attended to by the Christian as abstaining from pork is by the Jew.

Most of the particles of blood, when meat is boiled, rise in the form of scum; these should be carefully removed—but there are always stray particles left floating in the water, and when this liquor is strained through a sieve or cloth (a colander is not fine enough) there will be coagulated blood at the bottom in the form of sediment. After the liquor is thus purified, you can add whatever vegetables you choose—rice, carrots, cabbage, onions, and potatoes are all used. If the liquor is too much, boil it awhile uncovered and let it evaporate. If it require richness, you had better take some of the fat skimmed off—melt it in a saucepan with a spoonful of flour well stirred in—this unites with the fat, and prevents it from floating, like oil, on the top of the liquor. Then stir this mixture into the soup, add whatever flavors of seasoning you choose; pepper and sweet herbs are usually in favor.—Crackers, toasted or hard bread may be added a short time before the soup is wanted; but do not put in those libels on civilized cookery, called *dumplings!* One might about as well eat, with the hope of digesting, a brick from the ruins of Babylon, as one of the hard, heavy masses of boiled dough which usually pass under this name.

Indeed, it is, on many accounts, preferable, that bread should be eaten *with,* rather than *in,* our soups. In the former case, the bread assists to cool the broth, which is otherwise almost always taken *too hot*. Here is one great cause of disease to the stomach from this article of diet. Besides, hot liquors greatly injure the teeth; and also by passing immediately into the blood, and thus circulating through the whole system, cause an unnatural glow and perspiration which often predisposes to colds, and is weakening to delicate constitutions. When we are well, and wish to continue so, it is best never to take food or drinks warmer than new milk. In sickness, hot drinks are sometimes needed as stimulants.

MOCK TURTLE SOUP.*—Scald and clean thoroughly a calf's head with the skin on; boil it gently one hour in four quarts of water, skimming it well. Take out the head, and when almost cold, cut the meat off and divide it into bits about an inch square.

Slice and fry, of a light brown in butter, two pounds of the leg of beef, and two of veal, with five onions cut small, and two ounces of green sage. Add these to the liquor in which the head was boiled, also the bones of the head and trimmings, two whole onions, a handful of parsley, one teaspoonful of ground allspice and two of black pepper, salt to your taste, and the rind of one lemon; let it simmer and stew gently for five hours—then strain it, and when cold take off the fat. Put the liquor into a clean stewpan, add the meat cut from the head, and for a gallon of soup add half a pint of Madeira wine or claret, mix a spoonful of flour and a cup of butter with a little of the broth, and stir it in. Let it stew very gently till the meat is tender, which will be about an hour.

About twenty minutes before it is to be served, add a small tea-spoonful of Cayenne, the yolks of eight or ten hard-boiled eggs and a dozen force-meat balls; some add the juice of a lemon. When the meat is tender, the soup is done.

To make the meat balls, boil the brains for ten minutes, then put them in cold water; when cool, chop and mix them with five spoonfuls of grated bread, a little grated nutmeg,

* There is no use in a receipt for making the *real turtle*—that is so seldom done in a family.

pepper, salt and thyme and two eggs; roll the balls as large
as the yolk of an egg, and fry them of a light brown in butter or good dripping.

Very good soup in imitation of turtle is also made from
calves' feet. Four of these boiled in two quarts of water,
till very tender—the meat taken from the bones, the liquor
strained—a pint of good beef gravy and two glasses of wine
added, seasoned as the calves' head soup—with hard eggs,
balls, &c.

CURRIE SOUP.—Make about two quarts of strong veal
broth seasoned with two onions, a bunch of parsley, salt
and pepper; strain it, and have ready a chicken, cut in
joints and skinned; put it into the broth, with a table-spoonful of currie powder; boil the chicken till quite tender. A
little before serving, add the juice of a lemon, and stir in
a tea-cupful of cream. Serve boiled rice to eat with this
broth.

VEAL SOUP.—Skin four pounds of a knuckle of veal,
break, and cut it small, put it into a stewpan with two gallons of water; when it boils skim it, and let it simmer till
reduced to two quarts; strain, and season it with white pepper, salt, a little mace, a desert-spoonful of lemon juice, and
thicken it with a large table-spoonful of flour, kneaded with
an ounce of butter.

BEEF OR MUTTON SOUP.—Boil very gently in a closely
covered saucepan, four quarts of water, with two pounds
of beef cut in small pieces, or the same quantity of mutton
chops taken from the middle of the neck, and a half cup of
rice or bread crumbs; skim it well; season with pepper and
salt, add two turnips, two carrots, two onions, and one head
of celery, all cut small; let it stew with these ingredients four
hours, when it will be ready to serve.

WHITE SOUP.—Take a good knuckle of veal, or two or
three short shanks, boil it in four quarts of water about four
hours, with some whole white pepper, a little mace, salt, two
onions, and a small bit of lean ham; strain it, and when cold
take off all the fat and sediment; beat up six yolks of eggs
and mix them with a pint of good cream, then pour the boil-

ing soup upon it by degrees, stirring it well, and if it is liked, add the best part of the gristles.

N. B. Always boil cream before putting it in soup or sauce.

PIGEON SOUP.—Take eight pigeons, cut down two of the oldest, and put them with the necks, pinions, livers, and gizzards of the others, into four quarts of water; let it boil till the substance is extracted, and strain it; season the pigeons with mixed spices and salt, and truss them as for stewing; pick and wash clean a handful of parsley, chives or young onions, and a good deal of spinach, chop them; put these in a frying-pan with a quarter of a pound of butter, and when it boils, mix in a handful of bread crumbs, keep stirring them with a knife till of a fine brown; boil the whole pigeons till they become tender in the soup, with the herbs, and fried bread. If the soup be not sufficiently high seasoned, add more mixed spices and salt.

VEGETABLE SOUP.—Pare and cut small one dozen of common-sized onions, five large yellow turnips, two heads of celery, and three large carrots; wash and put them in a stew-pan with two ounces of butter, cover it closely; and when the vegetables are a little soft, add to them four quarts of well-seasoned gravy soup made of roast-beef bones, and let it stew four or five hours; rub it through a sieve, put it on the fire, boil and skim it before serving.

RICE SOUP.—Boil in four quarts of water the scrag end of a neck of veal and one pound of lean ham, till it is reduced nearly half; carefully skimming it, season with white pepper, and two blades of mace. Wash very clean three quarters of a pound of rice, strain the soup, and boil the rice in it till it is tender.

OLD PEASE SOUP.—Put a pound and a half of split peas on in four quarts of water, with roast-beef or mutton bones, and a ham bone, two heads of celery, and four onions, let them boil till the peas are sufficiently soft to pulp through a sieve, strain it, put it into the pot with pepper and salt, and boil it nearly one hour. Two or three handfuls of spinach, well washed and cut a little, added when the soup is strained, is a great improvement; and in the summer young green peas in the place of the spinach; a tea-spoonful of celery seed, or essence of celery, if celery is not to be had.

SOUP FOR AN INVALID.—Cut in small pieces one pound of beef or mutton, or part of both; boil it gently in two quarts of water; take off the scum, and when reduced to a pint, strain it. Season with a little salt, and take a tea-cupful at a time.

GRAVIES.

The French have a much greater variety of gravies than the English or Americans, who copy the English mode of cookery. Melted butter is with us the gravy for most meats. This is unnecessary, as nearly every kind of meat would yield gravy sufficient of its own; and we should thus have the flavor peculiar to each, if we cooked rightly. The French understand this, and their gravies are better as well as cheaper.

Butter, in the winter season, is always enormously dear, and it should be the study of the good housekeeper to dispense with it almost entirely when preparing meat.

When meat is roasted or stewed, the gravy should always be nicely freed from the fat, boiled and strained before it is sent to the table, to clear it from the coagulated blood; then thickened a little, if necessary, and flavored.

MELTED BUTTER.—Always use sweet butter; if in the least injured, it spoils the gravy. To make it of the best quality, cut two ounces of butter into little bits, put these in a clean stewpan, with a large tea-spoonful of flour and a table-spoonful of milk.

When thoroughly melted and mixed, add six table-spoonfuls of water, hold it over the fire, and shake it round every minute (all the time one way) till it just begins to simmer, then let it stand quietly and boil up. It should be of the thickness of good cream.

EGG SAUCE is made by putting two or three hard-boiled eggs, minced fine, into melted butter;—the butter need not be as thick when eggs are to be added.

PARSLEY AND BUTTER is made by adding parsley that

has been boiled a few minutes and chopped fine, to the melted butter.

WHITE SAUCE FOR BOILED FOWLS.—Melt in a tea-cupful of milk a large table-spoonful of butter, kneaded in a little flour; beat up the yolk of an egg with a spoonful of cream, stir into the butter, and put it over the fire, stirring it constantly; chopped parsley may be added.

CAPER SAUCE is made by adding one or two spoonfuls of capers to melted butter.

OYSTER SAUCE.—Beard and scald the oysters, strain the liquor, and thicken it with a little flour and butter, squeeze in a little lemon juice, and add three table-spoonfuls of cream. Heat it well, but do not let it boil.

BREAD SAUCE.—Boil a half pint of milk, and put into it a tea-cupful of bread crumbs, powdered; a small chopped onion which has been boiled in three waters, and let it simmer twenty minutes; then add a piece of butter as large as a walnut, boil up and serve.

TOMATA SAUCE.—Peel and slice twelve tomatas, picking out the seeds; add three pounded crackers; pepper and salt to your taste; stew twenty minutes.

CELERY SAUCE, *for boiled Fowls, Turkey, &c.*—Wash, pare and cut the celery in thin slices, about two inches long; it is better to be young. Stew it in a little weak gravy or water till tender; season with powdered mace, pepper and salt. Thicken with a good piece of butter kneaded in flour. The juice of a lemon may be added.

MINT SAUCE, *for hot or cold roast Lamb.*—Wash the mint, mince the leaves very fine, and mix them with vinegar and sugar. Lettuce is good prepared in the same manner.

CURRY SAUCE.—Mix curry powder with melted butter, and if wanted of a high flavor, add a little vinegar.

GRAVY SAUCE.—When beef is of good quality, and roasted with care, the gravy which flows from it, is the best sauce for the meat. Clear it of the fat and sediment, add a little salt, and if too thin, a dust of browned flour, and boil it up. To the gravy of veal, a little butter may be added.

CHAPTER V.

FISH AND CONDIMENTS.

Remarks on Fish—Cod—Salmon—Mackerel—Shad—Frying Fish—
Chowder—Shell fish—Oysters—Lobster—Condiments.

As food, fish is easier of digestion than meats are, with
the exception of salmon; this kind of fish is extremely
hearty food, and should be given sparingly to children, and
used cautiously by those who have weak stomachs, or who
take little exercise.

The small trout, found in rivers, are the most delicate and
suitable for invalids; lake fish are also excellent, and any
kind of fresh-water fish, if cooked immediately after being
caught, are always healthful.

But the ocean is the chief dependence for the fish-mar-
ket, and there is little danger (if we except salmon and
lobsters) that its kind of aliment will, in our country, be
eaten to excess. It would be better for the health of those
who do not labor, if they would use more fish and less flesh
for food. But then fish cannot be rendered so palatable,
because it does not admit the variety of cooking and flavors
that other animal food does.

Fish is much less nutritious than flesh. The white kinds
of fish, cod, haddock, flounders, white fish, &c., are the
least nutritious; the oily kinds, salmon, eels, herrings, &c.,
are more difficult to digest.

Shell fish have long held a high rank as restorative food;
but a well-dressed chop or steak is much better to recruit
the strength and spirits.

Cod, *whiting*, and *haddock*, are better for being a little
salted, and kept one day before cooking.

COD'S HEAD AND SHOULDERS, TO BOIL.—Wash it clean;
tie it up, and dry it with a cloth. Allow in the proportion
of every five measures of water, one of salt; when it boils,

take off the scum; put in the fish, and keep it boiling very fast for twenty-five or thirty minutes. Serve with the roe and milt parboiled, cut into slices and fried, and garnish with curled parsley and horse-radish. Sauces;—oyster, melted butter, or egg.

To CRIMP COD.—Cut a fresh cod into slices or steaks; lay them for three hours in salt and water, and a glass of vinegar; when they may be boiled, fried, or broiled, as you please.

COD SOUNDS.—These are reckoned a great delicacy; and may be either boiled, baked, roasted or broiled. Previous to cooking in any way, they must be well soaked, the black skin all picked off, and washed clean; then parboiled. If broiled, dust with flour, season with pepper and salt. Put a table-spoonful of catsup into a little melted butter for the gravy, or strew with bread crumbs and fry them.

To BOIL FRESH SALMON.—Salmon requires more boiling and in a larger quantity of water than any other kind of fish. It must be thoroughly done, or it is very unhealthy.

Make the water strong with salt, let it boil, skim and put in the salmon; continue to skim off all the scum that rises. A piece weighing half a pound requires fifteen minutes. Sauces—lobster, egg and butter.

To PICKLE SALMON.—To a quart of liquor the fish has been boiled in, put rather more than half a pint of vinegar, and half an ounce of whole black pepper; boil it, and when it is cold pour it over the fish previously laid in a deep dish.

This is a good way to dress the salmon left after a dinner. If you boil it purposely to pickle, do not remove the scales, it keeps better.

Pour a little sweet oil over the top of the pickle, and the fish will keep good for months.

To BROIL SALMON.—Cut it in slices about an inch and a half thick; dry it in a clean cloth; sprinkle over a little salt; put your gridiron over a clear but not very hot fire; when the bars are warm, rub them with sweet oil or lard; lay the salmon on, and when done on one side, turn it gently and broil the other.

To prepare *salted salmon* for broiling, soak it in *cold* water till freshened.

To BOIL MACKEREL.—The excellence of mackerel is to have it fresh as possible; it must be cleaned nicely; put it into sufficient water to cover it, (a little salt should be sprinkled in the water,) and let it rather simmer than boil. A small mackerel will be done in fifteen minutes. Do not allow them to stand in the water a moment after they are done.

Trout, perch and bass are boiled in the same manner.

Melted butter is used for boiled fish.

To BROIL MACKEREL.—Clean and split them open; wipe dry; lay them on a clean gridiron, rubbed with suet, over a very clear slow fire; turn; season with pepper, salt, and a little butter; fine-minced parsley is also used.

Trout and perch are broiled in the same way.

To BROIL A SHAD.—This is a delicate and delicious fish. Clean, wash, and split the shad, and wipe it dry; sprinkle it with pepper and salt, and broil it like mackerel.

To FRY COD OR OTHER FISH.—It is much more difficult to fry fish than meat.

Lard or dripping is better than butter, because the last burns so easily. The fat fried from salt pork is best of all.

The fire must be clear and hot, but not furious; the fat hot when the fish is put in, and there should be sufficient to cover the fish. Skim the fat before laying in the fish.

Cut the cod in slices half or three quarters of an inch thick; rub them with Indian meal to prevent breaking, fry it thoroughly.

Trout and perch are fried in the same manner; only do not rub Indian meal on them; dip in white of an egg and bread crumbs, or dust with flour.

To MAKE CHOWDER.—Lay some slices cut from the fat part of pork, in a deep stewpan, mix sliced onions with a variety of sweet herbs, and lay them on the pork; bone and cut a fresh cod into thin slices, and place them on the pork, then put a layer of pork, on that a layer of biscuit, then alternately the other materials until the pan is nearly full, season with pepper and salt, put in about a quart of water, cover the stewpan very close, and let it stand, with fire above as well as below, for four hours; then skim it well, and it is done.

This is an excellent dish and healthy, if not eaten *too hot*.

SHELL FISH.—Oysters and clams generally agree well with those who like them; but lobster must be eaten cautiously. It is very apt to disagree with delicate stomachs.

To FRY OYSTERS.—Make a batter as for pancakes, seasoned with grated nutmeg, white pepper and salt, and add some finely-grated bread crumbs; dip in the oysters and fry them of a light brown. Or dip them into the white of an egg beat up, then roll them in bread crumbs, seasoned with a little salt and pepper.

To STEW OYSTERS.—Open and take the liquor from them, cleanse them from grit, strain the liquor and add the oysters with a little mace and lemon-peel, a bit of butter rolled in flour, and a few white peppers. Simmer them very gently for eight or ten minutes. Toast thin slices of bread, lay these at the bottom of a dish and pour the oysters over.

To SCALLOP OYSTERS.—Take off the beards; stew them in their liquor strained, with a little mace, pepper and salt, fry some grated bread crumbs in a little butter, till of a nice brown; put the crumbs alternately with the oysters into a dish, and serve.

To STEW LOBSTERS.—A middling-sized lobster is best: pick all the meat from the shells and mince it fine; season with a little salt, pepper, and grated nutmeg; add three or four spoons of rich gravy and a small bit of butter. If you have no gravy, use more butter, and two spoonfuls of vinegar; stew about twenty minutes.

LOBSTER COLD.—It is frequently eaten in this way, with a dressing of vinegar, mustard, sweet oil, and a little salt and cayenne.

The meat of the lobster must be minced very fine; and care must be taken to *eat but a little* of this dish.

CONDIMENTS.

The fashions of cookery, as well as of dress, have changed very materially since the days of worthy Mrs. Glass,
whose receipts seem little else but a catalogue of herbs,
spices, essences, and all manner of flavors; a perfect " Magazine of Taste."

The crape cushion and periwig were not greater viola-
tions of the beauty of the natural hair and the comfort of
the individual, than was the deluge of condiments, then
thought indispensable to good cookery, to the pure taste of
the palate, and the real enjoyments of appetite.

We are just beginning to learn that the natural flavor of
every kind of animal and vegetable production, suitable for
food, is more delicate and exquisite, when properly prepared, than any which can be imparted by an incongruous
medley of seasoning. Still there are many improvements
to be made in the " art of cookery," before the perfection
of simplicity will be obtained; before we learn the right
process of dressing each kind of food, so as to retain all its
best nutriment and essence; or discover the appropriate
condiment and sauce for every dish.

To learn these things, we must study the natural laws
of the human constitution, and the arrangements of Providence. We find a great diversity of productions in the
different climates; and there is little danger of error in as-
suming the rule that each sort is most healthful and to be
used most freely, where it has been most plentifully provided by Nature. Thus, in the climate of the Greenlander,
oil and the fattest substances are necessary to sustain the
human constitution, nor is any condiment, or scarcely a
vegetable, required.

In the warm climates of the East, pepper and other spices are produced, and, no doubt, required, where the diet
is chiefly vegetable, or meats newly killed, and the stomach
and system are relaxed by the heat. It is the nature of all
kinds of spices, and high-seasoned food, to irritate, in a
degree, the lining or inner membrane of the stomach; and
they prove hurtful or healthful in proportion as this stimu-
lus is needed or not.

In our own climate, the season of the year, as well as the age and constitution of the individual, must be taken into the calculation. During the cold weather, more fat meats and richer gravies may be eaten, but few or no condiments, except a little salt, is needed.

In summer, fish, and a large proportion of vegetable diet, should be used; meats more sparingly, and sauces made with cream and eggs instead of butter; (this, when new, should be eaten chiefly in substance with bread) and then condiments are doubtless advantageous, if not too freely used.

For those who exercise much in the open air, and require very hearty food, pepper, mustard, and Cayenne may be beneficial because they provoke thirst; and a very large amount of water is required to be taken into the stomach to supply the waste of the blood by perspiration.

But do not *give high-seasoned food to children at any time.*

The common condiments, *salt, pepper, spices,* &c., are well known. A few receipts for mingling and preparing these will now be given.

MIXED SPICES AND SEASONINGS —Dry and pound fine one ounce of black pepper, of nutmeg, ginger and cinnamon, half an ounce each, and a dozen cloves. Mix and bottle the whole together; use for flavoring force-meats and gravies.

SEASONINGS FOR WHITE SAUCE, FRICASSEES, AND RAGOUTS.—White pepper, nutmeg, mace and lemon-peel, pounded together.

POWDER OF FINE HERBS for flavoring Soups and Sauces, when fresh herbs cannot be obtained.—Take dried parsley two ounces; of lemon-thyme, summer-savory, sweet marjorum and basil, one ounce each; dried lemon-peel one ounce; these must be dried thoroughly, pounded fine, the powder mixed, sifted, and bottled. You can add celery seeds if liked.

HORSE-RADISH POWDER.—In the beginning of winter, slice horse-radish, and dry it slowly before the fire. When dry, pound and bottle.

MUSHROOM POWDER.—Peel large, fleshy, button mush-rooms, and cut off the stems; spread them on plates, and dry them in a slow oven. When thoroughly dry, pound them with a little Cayenne and mace; bottle and keep the powder in a dry place. A tea-spoonful of this powder will give the mushroom flavor to a tureen of soup, or to sauce for poultry, hashes, &c.

All these powdered seasonings must be kept closely corked.

HOUSEHOLD VINEGARS.—Vinegar is an article perpetual-ly wanted in a family, and to buy it is expensive. The good housekeeper should prepare her own.

SUGAR VINEGAR.—To every gallon of water put two pounds of coarse brown sugar. Boil and skim this. Put it to cool in a clean tub; when about lukewarm, add a slice of bread soaked in fresh yeast. Barrel it in a week, and set it in the sun in summer or by the fire in winter, for six months, without stopping the bung-hole; but cover it with thin canvass or an inverted bottle to keep out the flies.

CIDER VINEGAR.—Put a pound of white sugar to a gal-lon of cider, and, shaking them well together, let them ferment for four months; a strong and well-colored vinegar will be the result.

FLAVORED VINEGARS.—These are a cheap and agreeable addition to sauces, hashes, &c. Infuse a hundred red chi-lies, fresh gathered, into a quart of good vinegar; let them stand ten days, shaking the bottle every day. A half ounce of Cayenne will answer the same purpose. This is good in melted butter for fish sauce, &c.

CELERY VINEGAR.—Pound a half ounce of celery seed, and steep it for ten days in a quart of vinegar; strain and bottle it.

HORSE-RADISH VINEGAR.—Pour a quart of strong vinegar, boiling hot, on three ounces of scraped horse-radish and a tea-spoonful of pounded black pepper, and half the quantity of Cayenne. Let it stand four days, tightly covered, then strain and put it in the cruet for use. It is good on cold roast-beef, and excellent in the gravy for chops, steaks, &c.

CUCUMBER VINEGAR.—Pare and slice ten large cucumbers, and steep them in three pints of the best vinegar for a few days. Strain and bottle it.

PICKLES are very indigestible things, and ought rarely to be eaten. They are chiefly valuable in cookery as affording flavored vinegar for seasonings. The above receipts of flavored vinegars will render pickles, for this purpose, unnecessary.

MUSTARD is best when freshly made. Mix by degrees the best ground mustard and a little fine salt with warm water; rub these a long time till perfectly smooth.

MILD MUSTARD.—Mix as above, but use milk instead of water, and sugar instead of salt.

CATSUPS.—Mushroom is most esteemed; but the difficulty in our country of obtaining the right kind of plant, (some are poisonous,) renders a receipt of little consequence. It is better to buy this catsup at the shops.

TOMATO CATSUP.— This is a very good and healthy flavor for meats, sauces, &c. Take two quarts of skinned tomatos, two table-spoonfuls of salt, two of black pepper, and two of ground mustard; also one spoonful of allspice, and four pods of red pepper. Mix and rub these well together, and stew them slowly in a pint of vinegar for three hours. Then strain the liquor through a sieve, and simmer down to one quart of catsup. Put this in bottles and cork tightly.

WALNUT CATSUP.—Thoroughly bruise one hundred and twenty young walnuts; put to them three quarters of a pound of fine salt and a quart of vinegar; stir them every day for a fortnight; then strain; squeeze the liquor from them through a cloth; add to this one ounce of whole black pepper, forty cloves, half an ounce of nutmeg bruised, half an ounce of ginger, and a few blades of mace. Boil the whole for half an hour; strain and bottle it for use.

CURRY POWDER.—Take four tea-spoonfuls of powdered white ginger, eight of coriander seeds, two of tumeric, and one of Cayenne; dry, pound and mix all well together, and keep in a glass bottle tightly corked.

CHAPTER VI.

VEGETABLES.

Importance of vegetable Food—Best manner of cooking—Potatoes—
Turnips—Cabbage—Onions—Beets—Carrots—Parsnips —Peas—
Beans—Squash—Cucumbers—Tomatos, &c.

THE importance of using a portion of vegetable food can hardly be overrated, though to make this our only diet does and must prove injurious, because contrary to man's nature and the arrangements of the Creator.

The farinaceous (or mealy) are far more nutritious than other vegetables ; but none are sufficiently so to sustain the constitution under the cares and labors necessary to the full development of the energies of body and mind. And unless these can be developed and sustained, the rational and moral character of the human race will never be perfected.

Still, though animal food is never, except in peculiar cases of disease, to be wholly abandoned, we must be quite as scrupulous not to neglect the vegetable part of our diet. This is necessary in order to prevent the concentrated diet of flesh from too sudden and stimulating action. Besides, our nature demands a portion of vegetables to keep the system in proper and healthy order. A *mixed diet* is the only right regimen—the proportions, of the different kinds of food, vary, with different ages and constitutions, in different climates, and seasons ; still, in some degree, this rule should never be abandoned.

The very young require a large portion of mild farinaceous vegetables—such as rice, sago, tapioca and potatoes ; the two first are very easy of digestion.

Potatoes contain much water, and therefore remain longer in the stomach ; for this reason they are not good for dyspeptics. Beans and peas, when well cooked, are healthy food for those who exercise much and eat considerable animal food. Vegetables require more attention in cooking than is generally bestowed. How often they are brought to table in a half raw or insipid state! Thus we have waxy, watery, or soddened potatoes, parboiled cabbage, and green peas so hard they might be used effectively as shot. If these dishes are eaten, they can hardly be digested; but they rarely are taken freely; the consequence is that too much meat is used at dinner. If the vegetables were only cooked properly, the appetite for them would be increased as well as the power of digestion.

There are three things to be attended to in cooking vegetables; make them sufficiently soft, develop their best flavor, and correct any rank or disagreeable taste they may have. These things are very easily accomplished—boil them sufficiently—change the water if they are rank or unpleasant—and add a little salt, sugar or spice, as the case may require.

Vegetables are always best when newly gathered—except the potato; that is better in winter, if well kept.

They are in greatest perfection when in greatest plenty, that is, in their proper season.

Except spinach, all vegetables should be boiled quickly (soft water is much the best) in an open vessel, and carefully skimmed.

POTATOES.

Potatoes should be kept in the cellar covered, and be carefully sprouted, as soon as the spring opens.

The middling-sized potatoes are best; the white mealy kind are better than the colored.

To boil Potatoes in the best manner, is a very great perfection in cookery. The following way is a good one. Take potatoes as nearly equal in size as possible, wash, but do not pare or cut them; put them into a pot, the largest potatoes at the bottom, cover them with cold water, and about one inch over. Too much water injures them very much. Throw in a spoonful of salt, and let them boil about five minutes, then take off the pot and set it where it will simmer slowly for thirty minutes—then try the potatoes with a fork; if it passes easily through, they are done; if not, let them simmer till they are; then pour off the water, place the pot where the potatoes will keep hot, but not burn, and let them stand, *uncovered,* till the moisture has evaporated. Then they are mealy and in perfection.

ANOTHER WAY TO BOIL POTATOES.—Pare, wash and throw them into a pan of cold water; then put them on to boil in a clean pot with cold water sufficient to cover them, and sprinkle over a little salt; let them boil slowly *uncovered* till you can pass a fork through them; pour off the water, and set them where they will keep hot till wanted. When done in this way, they are very mealy and dry.

Potatoes, either boiled or roasted, should *never be covered* to keep them hot.

TO ROAST POTATOES.—Choose all of a size, wash clean and rinse; put them on a tin, and bake them in a stove or Dutch oven. It takes more than an hour. Send them to the table with the skins on. They are excellent with cold meat, and healthy food for children, mashed with a little salt and gravy or cream.

MASHED POTATOES.—When old, potatoes are best *boiled and mashed,* with a little butter, salt and cream, or milk. They may be also sliced and fried raw, in hot salt-pork fat —or after they are boiled. Both dishes are relished. But a plain, boiled, or roasted potato, when well cooked, is the best and most healthy; and, though not a substitute for bread, it is one of the most useful vegetable productions.

TURNIPS should be pared; put into boiling water, with a little salt; boiled till tender; then squeeze them thoroughly from the water, mash them smooth, add a piece of butter and a little pepper and salt.

CABBAGE requires to be well washed before it is cooked; boil it in a large quantity of water, with a little salt, till it is soft and tender; skim the water carefully when it first boils. If the head is large, cut it—but a small head is the best.

ONIONS are best boiled in milk and water.

BEETS should be washed clean, but never cut—put in boiling water, and cooked till very tender.

CARROTS may be cut if too large; put in boiling water, with a little salt.

Parsnips must be washed and scraped very clean, boiled like carrots.

Green Peas should be young and fresh-shelled; wash them clean, put them on in plenty of boiling water, with a little salt and a tea-spoonful of pounded loaf sugar. Boil till tender.

Green peas are a most delicious vegetable when cooked enough, but half-done, hard things are very unhealthy. It takes from half an hour to an hour to boil them. Never let them stand in the water after they arc done. Season with a little butter and salt.

To stew young Peas and Lettuce.—Wash and make perfectly clean one or two heads of cabbage lettuce, pick off the outside leaves, and lay them for two hours in cold water with a little salt in it; then slice them, and put them into a sauce-pan, with a quart or three pints of peas, three table-spoonfuls of gravy, a bit of butter dredged with flour, some pepper and salt, and a tea-spoonful of pounded loaf sugar. Let them stew, closely covered, till the peas are soft.

Green Beans, or string beans as they are usually called, must be done till very tender—it takes nearly an hour and a half. Put them on in boiling water, after they have been prepared and well washed.

Greens of all kinds, spinach, beet-tops, &c. must be put in when the water boils.

Squash is a rich vegetable, particularly the yellow winter squash. This requires more boiling than the summer kind. Pare it, cut in pieces, take out the seeds and boil it in a very little water till it is quite soft. Then press out all the water, mash it and add a little butter, pepper and salt.

To stew Cucumbers.—Pare eight or ten large cucumbers, and cut them into thick slices, flour them well, and fry them in butter; then put them into a sauce-pan with a tea-cupful of gravy; season it with Cayenne, salt and catsup. Let them stew for an hour, and serve them hot.

To stew Tomatos.—Pour boiling water over them, then

take off the skins, and stew them slowly without water half an hour, adding a little salt and butter. This is said to be a very healthy vegetable.

To STEW OLD PEAS.—Put into a sauce-pan a pint of water, a slice of ham, a quart of old peas and a tea-spoonful of white sugar. Cover the pan closely, and let them stew two hours, or till tender. Take out the ham, and add a bit of butter rolled in flour.

To FRICASSEE FRENCH BEANS.—Boil one quart of beans till soft; strain off the water, put them in a sauce-pan with half a pint of sweet cream, a little salt and grated nutmeg, sprinkle over a little flour, and let them stew ten minutes.

CHAPTER VII.

PUDDINGS AND PIES.

Nature of this diet—Preparation of puddings—Arrow root—Sago—Tapioca—Rice—Batter—Potato—Bread—Custard—Apple—Damson—Lemon—Plum—Christmas Pies—Not healthy food—Paste for pies—Apple pie—Rhubarb—Fruit—Squash—Pumpkin—Custard—Tarts—Puffs—Mince pies

CONSIDERED in relation to health, there is not much to be said in favor of either of these kinds of diet, as usually managed; that is, taken after a full dinner of meat and vegetables. Many kinds of pudding are excellent and nutritious food; rice, sago and arrow-root, in particular; and if needed as food, nothing would be more healthy. The mischief is that these delicious compounds often tempt to repletion, which plain bread, cheese and fruit would not be so likely to do.

Dyspeptic people are generally injured by taking rich puddings or pies at any time. And there is a kind of pudding, made of fruit in *paste*, and boiled, which those who wish to avoid dyspepsia shonld never taste. No woman who regards her own health or that of her family, should ever allow a *dumpling or paste pudding* to be boiled in her house. I shall give no receipts for either. There is no way of *boiling* wheat *dough* which can render it fit for food; it will be crude and heavy, and lay hard in the stomach, unless a person has from nature or violent exercise, such a voracious appetite that, like the one described by Hood—" he could all but eat and digest himself."

Fruit mixed with batter, if rightly prepared, is far less objectionable; though this kind of pudding is not so nourishing or healthful as those made of rice, sago or Indian meal, baked. A boiled Indian pudding, if made nearly as thin as batter, is not very apt to be injurious; still made like hasty pudding it is more easily digested.

In preparing nice puddings, always beat the eggs very light, yolks and whites apart; the flour should be dried and sifted: if currants are used, they must be carefully picked, washed, and dried, and then dusted with flour before being put into the batter; raisins must be stoned; sugar dried and pounded; spices must be very fine, and all the ingredients thoroughly mixed. It is better to mix the pudding an hour or two before it is to be baked or boiled.

ARROW-ROOT PUDDING.—From a quart of new milk take a small tea-cupful, and mix it with two large spoonfuls of arrow-root. Boil the remainder of the milk, and stir it amongst the arrow-root; add when nearly cold, four well-beaten eggs, with two ounces of pounded loaf sugar, and the same of fresh butter broken into small bits; season with grated nutmeg. Mix it well together, and bake it in a buttered dish fifteen or twenty minutes.

SAGO PUDDING.—Boil five table-spoonfuls of sago, well picked and washed, in a quart of milk till quite soft, with a stick of cinnamon. Then stir in one teacup of butter and two of powdered loaf sugar. When it is cold, add four eggs well beaten, and a little grated nutmeg. Mix all well together, and bake it in a buttered dish about three quarters of an hour. Brown sugar, if dried, will answer very well to sweeten it.

TAPIOCA PUDDING.—Wash four large table-spoonfuls of

tapioca, and soak it for an hour in a little warm water; strain it through a sieve, and mix it with the well-beaten yolks of four, and the whites of two eggs, a quart of good milk, half a tea-spoonful of grated nutmeg, and sweeten it with sugar.   Bake it in a dish, with or without puff paste around the edges, one hour.

RICE PUDDING BAKED OR BOILED.—Wash in cold water and pick very clean six ounces of rice; boil it in one quart of milk, with a bit of cinnamon, very gently, till it is quite tender; it will take about an hour; be careful and stir it often.   Take it from the fire, pick out the cinnamon, and stir in a tea-cupful of sugar, half a cup of butter, three eggs well beaten, a little powdered nutmeg—stir it till it is quite smooth.   You can line a pie-dish with puff paste, or bake it in a buttered dish, which is better,—about three quarters of an hour will bake it.

If you wish it more like custard, add one more egg and half a pint of milk.

If you boil it, you can add whatever fruit you like,—three ounces of currants, or raisins, or apples minced fine; it will take an hour to boil it.

Serve with wine sauce or butter and sugar.

RICE BLANCMANGE.—Simmer a tea-cupful of whole rice in the least water possible, till it almost bursts, then add half a pint of good milk or thin cream, and boil it till it is quite a mash, stirring it the whole time it is on the fire, that it may not burn.   Dip a mould in cold water, and pour the hot rice in and let it stand till cold, when it will come easily out.

This dish may be eaten with cream and sugar, or custard and preserved fruits; raspberries are best.   It should be made the day before it is wanted.

It can be flavored with spices, lemon-peel, &c., and sweetened with a little loaf sugar; it is then very excellent.

ARROW-ROOT BLANCMANGE.—Dissolve a tea-spoonful of arrow-root in a little cold water, take one pint of new milk, and one pint of cream, boil it for a few minutes with six blades of mace, a nutmeg and lemon-peel pounded—then add a quarter of a pound of sugar, and boil all together for ten minutes. Strain it over the arrow-root, and stir it till it is cool—then wet the mould and pour it in ; it will be congealed when it is cold.

Rice Snow Balls.—Boil some rice in milk till it is swelled and soft ; pare and carefully scoop out the core of five or six good-sized apples, put into each a little grated lemon-peel and cinnamon ; place as much of the rice upon a bit of linen as will entirely cover an apple, and tie each closely. Boil them two hours, and serve them with melted butter, sweetened with sugar.

Batter Pudding.—Take six ounces of fine flour, a little salt, and three eggs ; beat it up well with a little milk, added by degrees till the batter is quite smooth; make it the thickness of cream ; put it into a buttered pie-dish, and bake three quarters of an hour ; or in a buttered and floured basin, tied over tight with a cloth : boil one hour and a half, or two hours.

Any kind of ripe fruit that you like may be added to the batter,—only you must make the batter a little stiffer Blueberries or finely-chopped apple are most usually liked.

Potato Pudding.—Boil three large mealy potatoes, mash them very smoothly, with one ounce of butter, and two or three table-spoonfuls of thick cream ; add three well-beaten eggs, a little salt, grated nutmeg, and a table-spoonful of brown sugar. Beat all well together, and bake it in a buttered dish, for half or three quarters of an hour in a Dutch oven. A few currants may be added to the pudding.

Plain Bread Pudding.—Pour a quart of boiling milk over four ounces of bread crumbs, cover it till cold, and mix with three well-beaten eggs, a tea-cup of sugar, and half the peel of a grated lemon, or a little pounded cinnamon ; bake it in a buttered dish, and serve with sweet sauce.

Custard Pudding.—Mix with one table-spoonful of flour, a pint of cream, or new milk, three eggs, a spoonful of rose water, one ounce of fresh butter broken in small bits ; sweeten with pounded loaf sugar, and add a little grated nutmeg.

Bake it in a buttered dish for half an hour. Before serving, you can strew over it pounded loaf sugar, and stick over it thin cut bits of citron if you wish it to look very rich.

RICH APPLE PUDDING.—Peel and core six very large apples, stew them in six table-spoonfuls of water, with the rind of a lemon; when soft, beat them to a pulp, add six ounces of good brown sugar, six well-beaten eggs, a pint of rich cream, and a tea-spoonful of lemon juice; line a dish with a puff paste, and when baked, stick all over the top thin chips of candied citron and lemon-peel.

LEMON PUDDING.—Boil in water, in a closely covered sauce-pan, two large lemons till quite tender; take out the seeds, and pound the lemon to a paste; add a quarter of a pound of pounded loaf sugar, the same of fresh butter beaten to a cream, and three well-beaten eggs; mix all together and bake it in a tin lined with puff paste; take it out, strew over the top grated loaf sugar.

PLUM PUDDING.—As Christmas comes but once a year, a rich plum pudding may be permitted for the feast, though it is not healthy food; and children should be helped very sparingly. The following is a good receipt:—

Chop half a pound of suet very fine; stone half a pound of raisins; half a pound of currants nicely washed and picked; four ounces of bread crumbs; four ounces of flour; four eggs well beaten; a little grated nutmeg; mace and cinnamon pounded very fine; a spoonful of salt; four ounces of sugar; one ounce candied lemon; same of citron.

Beat the eggs and the spices well together: mix the milk with them by degrees, then the rest of the ingredients; dip a fine, close linen cloth into boiling water, and place it in a hair sieve; flour it a little, then pour in the batter and tie it up, allowing a little room to swell; put it into a pot containing six quarts of boiling water; keep a tea-kettle of boiling water and fill up your pot as it wastes; be sure to keep it boiling at least six hours—seven would not injure it.

This pudding should be mixed an hour or two before it is put on to boil; it makes it taste richer.

CUSTARD SAUCE *for Rice, Bread, Sago, or Custard Puddings, or Fruit Pies.*—Stir a pint of sweet cream in a clean sauce-pan over coals, till it comes to a boil. Then mix into it the beaten yolks of two eggs, with two spoonfuls of finely pulverized sugar, and a piece of butter as large as a walnut; pour the mixture backwards and forwards from the sauce-pan to a basin to prevent its curdling, and let it just come to the eve of boiling, constantly stirring it. Grate nutmeg on the top before serving.

COLD SWEET SAUCE *for* **Puddings.**—Take equal quantities of butter and sugar; beat them together till they are perfectly smooth; add a little wine; make the mixture in a lump, and set it in a cool place for fifteen minutes: grate nutmeg over it.

PIES.

Pies are more apt to prove injurious to persons of delicate constitutions than puddings, because of the indigestible nature of the pastry.

Those who eat much of this kind of food, when made rich, (and poor pies are poor things indeed,) usually complain of the loss of appetite, and feel a disrelish for any but high-seasoned food. It would really be a great improvement in the matter of health, (and without that we cannot long enjoy pleasure or even comfort in good living) as well as evince superior nicety of taste, if people would eat their delicious summer fruits with good light bread instead of working up the flour with water and butter into a compound that almost defies the digestive powers, and baking therein the fruits, till they lose nearly all their fine original flavor. Apples are about the only fruit that seems intended for cooking; (pears and quinces are good to preserve;) the stone fruits, cherries, plums, &c. are absolutely ruined by it; and nearly all the summer berries are injured by baking. And yet women *will make* pies; and mothers *will give* them to their young children, when a bowl of bread and milk, with a little ripe fruit in it, would satisfy their unvitiated appetites better, and in every respect do them much more good. Pies are best for winter food, because then we can bear a rich concentrated diet, better than during the hot weather. In the spring and summer, when milk and eggs are plenty and fresh, we should use custards and all the light farinaceous puddings; and ripe fruits. In cold weather, there is less danger of injury from mince pies and plum puddings; still, for the sedentary, the delicate, or dyspeptic, they are never safe.   And if the mistress of a family be a " good housekeeper"—that is, if she thoroughly understand the nature of food and the effect of its various combinations on the health of those for whom her table is spread, she will not permit the appearance of those kinds which can scarcely be taken by the strong and healthy without injury, and which are sure to prove hurtful to the young, weak, or invalid.

In making paste, particular care must be taken that the board, rolling-pin, cutters, &c. are very clean and dry.

The flour used should always be of the best quality, dried and sifted.

If the butter is very salt, it should be washed several times.   Never use *bad butter* in pastry—it spoils it.

Puff Paste.—Weigh equal quantities of flour and butter, rub rather more than the half of the butter into the flour, then add as much cold water as will make it into a stiff paste; work it until the butter be completely mixed with the flour, make it round, beat it with the rolling-pin, dust it, as also the rolling-pin, with flour, and roll it out towards the opposite side of the slab, or paste-board, making it of an equal thickness; then with the point of a knife put little bits of butter all over it, dust flour over and under it, fold in the sides and roll it up, dust it again with flour, beat it a little, and roll it out, always rubbing the rolling-pin with flour, and throwing some underneath the paste, to prevent its sticking to the board.   If the butter is not all easily put in at the second time of rolling out the paste, the remainder may be put in at the third; it should be touched as little as possible with the hands.

Tart Paste.—Rub into half a pound of flour, six ounces of butter and a table-spoonful of powdered loaf sugar; make it into a stiff paste with hot water.

Short Paste for Fruit Pies.—Rub into three quarters of a pound of flour a quarter of a pound of lard and a spoonful of grated sugar.   Make it into a paste with milk, roll it out, and add a quarter of a pound of butter. For a fruit tart it must be rolled out half an inch thick.

RAISED CRUST.—Melt in one pint of water one pound of lard; put four pounds of flour in a pan and sprinkle over a large spoonful of salt, and when the water and lard are hot, stir it with a spoon among the flour. When well mixed, work it with the hands till it is a stiff paste, when it is fit for use.

APPLE PIE.—Apples of a pleasant sour, and fully ripe, make the best pies—pare, core and slice them, line a deep buttered dish with paste, lay in the apples, strewing in moist brown sugar and a little pounded lemon-peel or cinnamon; cover and bake about forty minutes. The oven must not be very hot.

When apples are green, stew them with a very little water before making your pie. Green fruit requires a double quantity of sugar.

Gooseberries and green currants are made in the same manner.

RHUBARB PIES.—In England they call this "Spring fruit," which is a much more *relishing name than rhubarb.*

Peel off the skin from the young green stalks, and cut these into small pieces—put them in the pie with plenty of brown sugar, you can hardly put in too much. Cover the pie, and bake like apple.

You may stew the "Spring fruit" very soft, and make tarts.

FRUIT PIES.—When making pies from ripe summer fruits, such as raspberries, blueberries, cherries, damsons, &c. always take a deep plate, line it with paste, place a teacup, inverted in the middle, and fill the pie with fruit, a good quantity of brown sugar, with very little spice or seasoning. The cup is placed to receive the juice, which will flow from the fruit as they bake, and which would otherwise ooze out at the edges. It will all settle under the cup, which must be removed when the pie is cut open.

It is a pity to make these ripe fruits into pies; they would be so much healthier eaten with bread than pie-crust; still they are harmless compared with *meat pies, which should never be made.*

SQUASH PIE.—Pare, take out the seeds and stew the squash till very soft and dry. Strain or rub it through a sieve or colander. Mix this with good milk till it is thick as batter : sweeten it with sugar. Allow three eggs to a quart of milk, beat the eggs well, add them to the squash, and season with rose water, cinnamon, nutmeg, or whatever spices you like. Line a pie-plate with crust, fill and bake about an hour.

PUMPKIN PIE.—Stew the pumpkin dry, and make it like squash pie, only season rather higher. In the country, where this *real yankee pie* is prepared in perfection, ginger is almost always used with other spices. There too, part cream instead of milk, is mixed with the pumpkin, which gives it a richer flavor.

Roll the paste rather thicker than for fruit pies, as there is only one crust. If the pie is large and deep, it will require to bake an hour in a brisk oven.

CUSTARD PIE.—Beat seven eggs, sweeten a quart of rich milk, that has been boiled and cooled—a stick of cinnamon or a bit of lemon-peel should be boiled in it—sprinkle in a salt-spoon of salt, add the eggs, and a grated nutmeg, stirring the whole together.

Line two deep plates with good paste, set them in the oven three minutes to harden the crust ; then pour in the custard and bake twenty minutes.

CUSTARD TART.—Line a deep plate with puff paste ; have ready six or eight middling-sized apples, pared and the cores taken out. They should be mellow and pleasant. Put into each apple any kind of preserve you have, or a bit of sugar flavored. Now fill the dish with rich custard and bake it about half an hour.

Make in the same manner without crust—it is then called " Custard Pudding."

TARTS OF PRESERVED FRUITS.—Cover patty-pans, or shallow tins or dishes, with light puff paste, and lay the preserve in them, cover with light cross bars of puff paste, or with paste stars, leaves, or flowers. For the most delicate preserves, the best way is to bake the paste first, then put in the preserves, and ornament with leaves, baked for the purpose, on tins.

Puffs.—Roll out puff paste nearly a quarter of an inch thick, and, with a small saucer, or tin cutter of that size, cut it into round pieces; place upon one side raspberry or strawberry jam, or any sort of preserved fruit, or stewed apples; wet the edges, fold over the other side, and press it round with the finger and thumb. Or cut the paste into the form of a diamond, lay on the fruit, and fold over the paste, so as to give it a triangular shape.

Mince Pies.—The custom of eating mince pies at Christmas, like that of plumb puddings, was too firmly rooted for the " Pilgrim fathers" to abolish ; so it would be vain for me to attempt it. At Thanksgiving too, they are considered indispensable ; but I may be allowed to hope that during the remainder of the year, this rich, expensive and exceedingly unhealthy diet will be used very sparingly by all who wish to enjoy sound sleep or pleasant dreams.

The dyspeptic should always avoid them as he would his bane, and for children they should be forbidden food ; so tempting is the taste, that the only security consists in not tasting. So the " good housekeeper" will be careful not to place the temptation too often before her family.

Rich Mince Meat.—Cut the root off a neat's tongue, rub the tongue well with salt, let it lie four days, wash it perfectly clean, and boil it till it becomes tender ; skin, and when cold, chop it very finely. Mince as small as possible two pounds of fresh beef suet from the sirloin, stone and cut small two pounds of bloom raisins, clean nicely two pounds of currants, pound and sift half an ounce of mace and a quarter of an ounce of cloves, grate a large nutmeg ; mix all these ingredients thoroughly, together with one pound and a half good brown sugar. Pack it in jars.

When it is to be used, allow, for the quantity sufficient to make twelve small mince pies, five finely-minced apples, the grated rind and juice of a large lemon, add a wine glass and a half of wine ; put into each a few bits of citron and preserved lemon-peel.

Three or four whole green lemons, preserved in good brown sugar, and cut into thin slices, may be added to the mince meat.

FAMILY MINCE PIES.—Boil three pounds of lean beef till tender, and when cold chop it fine. Chop two pounds of clear beef suet and mix the meat, sprinkling in a table-spoonful of salt.

Pare, core and chop fine six pounds of good apples; stone four pounds of raisins and chop them; wash and dry two pounds of currants; and mix them all well with the meat. Season with powdered cinnamon one spoonful, a powdered nutmeg, a little mace and a few cloves pounded, and one pound of brown sugar—add a quart of Madeira wine and half a pound of citron cut into small bits. This mixture, put down in a stone jar and closely covered, will keep several weeks. It makes a rich pie for Thanksgiving and Christmas.

PLAIN MINCE PIES.—Take two pounds of lean beef boiled and one pound of suet, chopped fine; three pounds of apples, two pounds of raisins or currants, one pound of sugar, a little salt, pepper, cinnamon, cloves, and one nutmeg—moisten with new cider or sweet cream. Make a good paste, and bake about an hour.

The currants must be washed and dried at the fire; raisins stoned and chopped.

CHICKEN PIE.—Pick, clean, and singe the chickens; if they are very young, keep them whole, if large, cut them in joints, and take off the skin, wash them well, parboil in a pint of water, season them with salt, white pepper, grated nutmeg and mace mixed, and if whole, put into them a bit of butter rolled in flour, and a little of the mixed spices; lay them into a dish with the livers, and gizzards, and hearts well seasoned, add the gravy and yolks of five hard-boiled eggs; cover with a puff paste, and bake it for an hour.

Slices of cold ham and force-meat balls may be added to this pie. Or wash in cold water two or three ounces of macaroni, break it into small bits, simmer it for nearly half an hour in milk and water, drain and put it with the chickens into the dish, and also an ounce of butter.

CHAPTER VIII.

F R U I T S ,   P R E S E R V E S ,   E T C .

Nature of Fruits—Best times of using them—Ripe and fresh—
Cooked—Preserves—Jellies—Custards—Creams, &c.

FRUITS were the diet first allowed man; and it seems that the Eden taste still lingers in our race, for in childhood there is no food so eagerly sought and relished. But nothing which earth produces has escaped the curse, or rather mankind, by the excitement and indulgence of a depraved appetite, often convert the blessings and bounty of heaven into sources of disease and disquiet.

That fruits are naturally healthy in their season, if rightly taken, no one, who believes that the Creator is a kind and beneficent being, can doubt. And yet the use of summer fruits appears often to cause most fatal diseases, especially in children. Why is this? Because we do not conform to the natural laws in using this kind of diet. These laws are very simple and easy to understand.—Let the fruit be ripe when you eat it; and eat it when you require *food*.

Now, nearly one half of the summer fruits used are eaten in an unripe or decaying state; more than half sold in the cities are in this condition. And this unhealthy fruit is often taken when no food is needed, after the full dinner, or for pastime in the evening. It is given to children to amuse them or stop their crying, when they are often suffering from repletion. Is it a wonder that fruits make people and children sick under such circumstances?

In the country, fruits in their season usually form part of the morning and evening meal of children with bread and milk; fresh gathered fruits; and they seldom prove injurious eaten in this manner. Indeed, though far the greatest quantity of fruit is eaten in the country, and some in an unripe state, yet very little, comparatively, is used when it is decaying   And hence it doubtless is, that the diseases which so fatally afflict children in the cities, during the fruit season, are seldom of much consequence in the country.

The fruits sold in the city almost always are gathered in an unripe state, in order the better to bear the delay and disturbance of bringing to market ; they are therefore in that most crude and unhealthy condition,—"rotten (or at least decaying) before they are ripe," and all their best qualities are lost. Do not give such fruit to your young children. If it be possible, send or go with them into the country, during the fruit season, and let them ramble over the green hills and through the wide pastures, where, in the grass or by the rough fences, grow those delicious fruits, the raspberry, or blackberry, and strawberry, and pick for themselves. There they will scarcely be persuaded to eat an unripe or decaying berry. If you cannot do this, keep such fruits as much as possible from their knowledge ; for though it is undoubtedly of essential benefit to the health to use ripe fruits in the hot season, yet it is better to do without them entirely, than to eat them when utterly unfit for the stomach.*

Stone fruits are still more objectionable, because the stones and skins frequently swallowed by children are entirely indigestible. Peach skins are very unhealthy, and should never be eaten. In the southern cities, many bowel complaints are caused by the use of this fruit.

Apples and winter pears are very excellent food for children, indeed for almost any person in health ; but best when eaten at breakfast or dinner. If taken late in the evening, fruit often proves injurious. The old saying that apples are *gold in the morning, silver at noon, and lead at night,* is pretty near the truth. Both apples and pears are often good and nutritious when baked or stewed, for those delicate constitutions that cannot bear raw fruit.

Much of the fruit, gathered when unripe, might be rendered fit for food by preserving in sugar. This is an expen-

* It appears to me that the summer sickness among children is often caused by their eating too much meat, rich cakes, and high-seasoned, hearty food. During the hot months, they should eat mostly light cold bread, rice, milk, custards, &c., with *good ripe* fruits.

sive article of diet, if freely used, and therefore there is less danger that people will indulge to excess.

I would not recommend sweetmeats or fruit sauces at every meal; but a portion of these delicate preparations are healthy and economical; they decorate the table, and give zest to the evening meal of plain bread and butter, when otherwise rich cakes would be craved. Eaten with custards or rice, preserves or ripe berries are excellent in the summer season, when such kinds of food, nutritious, yet mild and light, are essential to the comfort of the sedentary, indeed of all, except those who exercise much in the open air.

The following receipts for this kind of cookery, which is truly a lady's department, are those combining most fully pleasantness of taste with economy and suitableness for family use.

Fruit for preserves is better not to be over-ripe; gather it on a *dry* day, and *after* a dry day if possible.

Good sugar is cheaper in the end than poor for this use; but for family preserves, if loaf or good lump sugar is used, it need not be clarified. Much time and waste of sugar is thus spared.

To boil Sugar.—To every pound of sugar allow one gill of water; stir it over the fire till the sugar is entirely dissolved; when it first boils up, pour in a very little cold water, and when it boils the second time, take it off the fire; let it settle ten minutes, carefully skim it, and boil it for half an hour, or till it will candy, and then put in the fruit.

Very good preserves for family use are made with brown sugar.

If you wish to clarify the sugar, add the white of one egg, well beaten, to every three pounds of sugar.

The preserving pans must be very clean.

The rule is to allow a pound of sugar to a pound of fruit; if to be kept for several months, this proportion is necessary; to use in the family, three quarters of a pound of sugar to a pound of fruit is sufficient.

Cherries should be stoned, and berries picked over very carefully.

RASPBERRY JAM.—Weigh equal proportions of pounded loaf (or lump) sugar and raspberries; put the fruit in a preserving pan, and with a silver spoon, or flat wooden stick, bruise and mash it well; let it boil up, then add the sugar, stirring it well with the fruit; when it boils, skim it, and then boil fifteen or twenty minutes.

STRAWBERRY JAM is made in the same way.

PEACH JAM.—Gather the peaches when quite ripe, peel and stone them; put them into a preserving pan, and mash them over the fire till hot; rub them through a sieve, and add to a pound of pulp the same weight of pounded loaf sugar, and half an ounce of bitter almonds, blanched and pounded; let it boil ten or twelve minutes, stir and skim it well.

TO PRESERVE DAMSONS.—To every pound of damsons allow three quarters of a pound of powdered sugar; put into jars or well-glazed earthen pots, alternately a layer of damsons, and one of sugar; tie strong paper or cloth over the pots, and set them in the oven after the bread is drawn; and let them stand till the oven is cold. The next day, strain off the syrup, and boil it till thick; when it is cold, put the damsons into small jars or glasses, pour over the syrup, which should cover them, and tie a wet bladder or strong cloth over them.

BLACK BUTTER.—This is a very nice preserve to spread on bread for children, and much healthier in the winter than salt butter. Take any kind of berries, currants, or cherries, (the latter must be stoned;) to every pound of fruit allow half a pound of sugar, and boil till it is reduced one fourth.

TO PRESERVE QUINCES.—Pare the quinces very thin, cut them in quarters, and to every five pounds of fruit put three pounds of sugar and half a pint of water; cover them to keep in the steam, and let them simmer gently for three hours. Or they may be preserved whole.

BAKED PEARS.—Take a pound of fine pears; peel, cut them in halves, and take out the cores; put them into a pan with a few cloves, half a pound of sugar, and some water. Set them in a moderate oven till tender, then put them on a slow fire to stew gently; add grated lemon-peel.

STEWED PEARS.—Slice and stew a small beet root in a pint of water; take out the beet; pare, core, and quarter your pears, and stew in the same water; sweeten to your taste, and add a little lemon-peel.

PRESERVED APPLES.—Weigh equal quantities of good brown sugar and of apples; peel, core, and mince them small. Boil the sugar, allowing to every three pounds a pint of water; skim it well, and boil it pretty thick; then add the apples, the grated peel of one or two lemons, and two or three pieces of white ginger; boil till the apples look clear and yellow. This preserve will keep for years.

CLEAR APPLES.—Boil half a pound of loaf sugar in a pint of water, take off the scum, and put in some large apples, pared, cored, and cut into quarters, with the peel and juice of a lemon: let them boil till clear, without a cover upon the saucepan.

TO STEW FRUIT.—The best way to stew any kind of fruit is to put the quantity you wish to cook into a wide-mouthed jar, with enough brown sugar to sweeten it; then cover the jar close, set it in a kettle of cold water, and boil it till the fruit is tender. This preserves the flavor of the fruit.

APPLE SAUCE.—In the country it is thought almost as indispensable to provide the stock of apple sauce for winter use as the pork; and there is no doubt of the healthiness as well as pleasantness of fruit taken in this way as food. To eat with meat, it is best made of sour apples, not too mellow, but pleasant flavored. Boil down new sweet cider till it is nearly as thick, when cold, as molasses; strain it through a sieve; wash the kettle, (it must be brass, or iron tinned;) put in the syrup, and as soon as it boils, put in the apples, which must have been previously pared, quartered, and cored. Stew over a slow fire of coals till very tender.

A barrel of cider will make half a barrel of very strong apple sauce, which will keep through the winter.

If you like it sweet to eat with tea, use sweet apples, and skim out the whole quarters, when soft; then boil the syrup and pour over them.

CURRANT JELLY.—Strain the juice of currants; add a pound and a quarter of sugar to every pint of juice. Boil it gently till it is clear, skimming it all the time. Raspberry, strawberry, &c. are made in the same manner.

To PRESERVE PUMPKINS.—Choose a thick yellow pumpkin which is sweet; pare, take out the seeds, and cut the thick part into any form you choose—round, square, egg-shaped, stars, wheels, &c.; weigh it; put it into a stone jar or deep dish, and place it in a pot of water to boil, till the pumpkin is so soft that you can pass a fork through it. The pot may be kept uncovered, and be sure that no water boils into the jar.

Take the weight of the pumpkin in good loaf sugar; clarify it, and boil the syrup with the juice of one lemon to every pound of sugar, and the peel cut in little squares. When the pumpkin is soft, put it into the syrup, and simmer gently about an hour, or till the liquor is thick and rich, then let it cool, and put it in glass jars well secured from air. It is a very rich sweetmeat.

To KEEP PRESERVES, JELLIES, &c.—Put the preserves, &c. in glass, china, or stone jars. *Glass* is much the best. Cover the top with white paper dipped in hot clarified *sugar*, (which is far better than *rum* or *brandy*,) after sprinkling the top of the preserves, &c. with sugar. Then cover close, and exclude the air entirely, and keep them in a dry place.

CRANBERRY AND RICE JELLY.—Boil and press the fruit, strain the juice, and, by degrees, mix into as much ground rice as will, when boiled, thicken to a jelly; boil it gently, stirring it, and sweeten to your taste. Put it in a basin or form, and serve to eat with cream.

ARROW-ROOT JELLY.—Steep for some hours in two tablespoonfuls of water, the peel of a lemon, and three or four bitter almonds pounded; strain, and mix it with three tablespoonfuls of arrow-root, the same quantity of lemon-juice, and one of wine; sweeten, and stir it over the fire till quite thick, and when quite cold, put it into jelly glasses.

WHOLE RICE IN A SHAPE.—Wash a large teacupful of rice in several waters, put it into a saucepan with cold water to cover it, and when it boils, add two cupfuls of rich milk, and boil it till it becomes dry; put it into a shape, and press it in well. When cold, turn it out, and serve with preserved currants, raspberries, or any sort of fruit round it.

ARROW-ROOT CREAM.—Mix a table spoonful of arrow-root with a teacupful of cold water; let it settle, and pour the water off. Sweeten and boil a quart of milk with the peel of a lemon and some cinnamon; pick them out, and pour it boiling upon the arrow-root, stirring it well and fre-quently till it is cold. Serve in a glass or china dish, with or without grated nutmeg on the top. It may be eaten with any preserved fruit, or fruit tarts.

CREAM FOR FRUIT TART.—Boil a stick of cinnamon, two or three peach leaves, or a few bruised almonds, in a quart of milk; strain, sweeten and mix it when cool, with three or four well-beaten eggs; stir it constantly over the fire till it thickens. It may be eaten with stewed apples, prunes, damsons, or any other fruit.

RED CURRANT, OR PINK CREAM.—Squeeze three quarters of a pint of juice from red currants when full ripe, add to it rather more than a quarter of a pound of pounded loaf sugar, and the juice of one lemon; stir it into a pint and a half of cream, and whisk it till quite thick. Serve it in a glass dish, or in jelly glasses. It may be made with currant jelly, which mix with the lemon juice and sugar.

Raspberry and strawberry cream may be made in the same way.

APPLE CREAM.—Peel and core five large apples; boil them in a little water, till soft enough to press through a sieve; sweeten, and beat with them the whisked whites of five eggs. Serve it with cream poured round it.

WHITE LEMON CREAM.—Boil the thin peel of two lemons in a pint of cream; strain and thicken it with the well-beaten yolks of three and whites of four eggs; sweeten with pounded loaf sugar; stir till nearly cold, and put it into glasses.

CUSTARD.—Sweeten a quart of good cream or good milk with pounded sugar; boil it with a bit of cinnamon and half the peel of a lemon; strain it, and when a little cooled, mix it gradually with the well-beaten yolks of ten eggs;

stir it over a slow fire till it is pretty thick; pour it into a basin, and add a table-spoonful of rose water; keep stirring it every now and then; put it into glasses, cups, or a dish. It may be made the day before it is wanted.

LEMON CUSTARD.—Put the juice of four lemons with three ounces of pounded loaf sugar into a deep dish. Boil the grated peel of one lemon and two ounces of sugar in a quart of cream, and pour it over the sugar and juice. Stir it well. It will keep several days.

ORANGE CUSTARD may be made in the same manner.

BAKED CUSTARD.—Boil a pint of thin cream with mace and cinnamon, or peach leaves; when cold, add three eggs, well beaten, a little rose-water and nutmeg; sweeten to your taste, and bake in china cups.

RICE CUSTARD.—Mix a pint of milk, half a pint of cream, one ounce of sifted ground rice, five or six bitter almonds, blanched and pounded with two table-spoonfuls of rose-water; sweeten with loaf sugar, and stir it all together till it nearly boils; add the well-beaten yolks of three eggs; stir, and let it simmer for about a minute; pour it into a dish, or serve it in cups, with sifted loaf sugar over the top.

TO ORNAMENT CUSTARDS OR CREAMS.—Whisk for one hour the whites of two eggs, together with two table-spoonfuls of raspberry, or red currant syrup or jelly; lay it in any form upon a custard or cream, piled up to imitate rock. It may be served in a dish with cream round it.

TO FREEZE CREAMS AND JELLIES.—Break ice, in a tub or bucket, in small pieces, and strew a handful of salt among it. Place your mould on this ice, and heap ice around it; take care the cream or jelly is quite cold before it is placed in ice. When taken out, dip a towel in hot water, and rub it quickly round the mould to detach the cream; then turn it carefully out.

Strawberry Ice Cream.—Mix one pound of strawberry juice, strained and sweetened, with one pint of whipped cream; if to be frozen in a mould, add a little isinglass, melted and strained. If to be eaten in glasses, isinglass is not necessary.

CHAPTER IX.

CAKES.

Remarks on Cake—Manner of making—Various kinds—Sponge cake—Seed—Macaroons—Kisses—Sugar drops—Rice—Rice cakes with butter—Caraway—Sugar—Tea—Gingerbread—Light cake —Composition—-Tunbridge—-German puffs—Common plum— Rich—Pound—Heart—Iceing for cakes—Warm cakes for breakfast and tea.

CAKE is one of the luxuries of the table, and, like all luxuries, must be sparingly indulged in order to be enjoyed, its value depending chiefly on its rarity. If gold were plenty as granite, it would be little prized; and were cakes used freely as bread, it would not only prove injurious to the constitution, but we would soon tire of the luscious compound.

As a delicacy at the tea-table, occasionally introduced, cake is not objectionable, unless made very rich with butter. The common gingerbread and several varieties of the cheap and simple cakes, which will be given in this work, are much better, as a part of the evening meal, than hot biscuit, or even a full supper of cold bread and butter in the winter season, when butter is usually too salt to be healthful.

But never spread butter on cake: it is a sin against that economy and propriety which domestic rules should always exhibit; and, besides, it renders the cake too rich for the stomach.

The kinds of cake most apt to prove injurious are pound cake and rich plum cake; but very little of these should ever be eaten, and if they could be wholly superseded by the *sponge cake* and other light varieties, it would be much better for the health of those who are in the habit of frequenting parties. Sponge cake, or those made in a similar manner, chiefly of eggs, sugar and flour, beaten light and well baked, would rarely prove injurious, if not eaten immoderately.

It will be well, however, always to bear in mind, that cake of every sort is to be partaken of as a luxury, not eaten for a full meal.   Those who attend evening parties several times in a week, can hardly take too small a quantity of the sweet and rich preparations.   Many a young lady loses her appetite bloom and health by indulgence in these tempting but pernicious delicacies;   and dyspeptic complaints frequently are aggravated, if not originated, by the absurd fashion of making our evening circles places for eating and drinking, rather than social and mental enjoyment.   They manage these things better in Paris.

Those ladies who live in the country must make their own cake; but for those who dwell in cities it is usually cheaper to buy it ready made for parties; then it is sure to be of good quality; and, as the quantity needed can be pretty accurately calculated, it will not be so expensive as to bake it at home, where considerable waste in the kitchen must be expected.

In preparing cake, the flour should be dried before the fire, sifted and weighed; currants washed and dried; raisins stoned; sugar pounded, and rolled fine and sifted; and all spices, after being well dried at the fire, pounded and sifted.

Almonds should be blanched, which is done by pouring hot water over them, and after standing some minutes taking off the skins, then throwing them into cold water.   When not pounded, they should be cut lengthwise into thin bits. Lemon and orange-peel must be pared very thin, and pounded with a little sugar.

Butter, after being weighed, should be laid in cold water, or washed in rose water; if salt, wash it well in several waters.

The yolks and whites of eggs should always be separately beaten in making nice cake, and strained.   First weigh or measure the ingredients; then sift the flour; powder the sugar; grind the spice; prepare the fruit; stir the butter and sugar together ; and the last thing beat the eggs.

SPONGE CAKE.—Take one pound of finely-pulverized loaf sugar, nine eggs, and twelve ounces of dried and sifted flour.   Beat the eggs, yolks and whites separately, nearly half an hour; then beat the sugar with the eggs till the whole is of a foam, have the oven ready, and stir in the flour lightly, adding a grated nutmeg and a little cinnamon or mace, then put the mixture in buttered tins filled only half full, and bake about half an hour; if in one large cake, it will require one hour. The oven should be quick—that is, just heated, but not so hot as to scorch.

LEMON SPONGE CAKE.—Take one pound of dried flour, three quarters of a pound of finely-pounded loaf sugar, seven eggs, the yolks and whites beaten separately, the grated peel and juice of a lemon, a table-spoonful of rose water; beat all for an hour with the hand; butter a tin, line it with a paper also buttered, put in the cake, and sift pounded sugar over the top. Bake it for an hour.

SEED CAKES.—Take one pound of flour; twelve ounces of lump sugar, pounded fine; seven eggs well beaten with the sugar; one ounce of caraway seeds dried and pounded, and two large table-spoonfuls of sour cream, with a tea-spoonful of pearlash. Bake an hour, if in one cake; in small tins, fifteen minutes.

MACAROONS.—Beat to a froth the whites of eight eggs, then add two pounds of finely-pounded and sifted loaf sugar, one pound of blanched sweet almonds, which must be pounded to a paste with rose water. Beat all these together till they become a thick paste, then drop it from a spoon upon a buttered tin. Place the drops a little apart, as they may spread. Bake them about ten minutes in a moderate oven.

KISSES.—Beat the whites of four eggs till they stand alone. Then beat in, gradually, a pound of finely-powdered sugar, a tea-spoonful at a time. Add eight drops of the essence of lemon, and beat the whole very hard.

Lay a wet sheet of paper on the bottom of a square tin pan. Drop on it, at equal distance, small tea-spoonfuls of stiff currant jelly. Put a little of the beaten egg and sugar at first, under the currant jelly. With a large spoon, pile some of the beaten white of egg and sugar, on each lump of jelly, so as to cover it entirely. Drop on the mixture as evenly as possible, so as to make the kisses of a round, smooth shape.

Set them in a cool oven, and as soon as they are colored,

they are done. Then take them out, and place the two bottoms together. Lay them lightly on a sieve, and dry them in a cool oven, till the two bottoms stick fast together so as to form one ball or oval.

SUGAR DROPS.—Beat the whites and yolks of four eggs separately to a light foam; dilute the yolks with two tea-spoonfuls of water, and turn them with the whites, and beat them some time; then add by degrees a pound of sugar in fine powder, and then four ounces of superfine flour, beating the mixture constantly. Drop the mixture on white paper placed in a tin plate, in any shape you please, ice them over with sugar in powder to prevent running, and bake about ten minutes in a moderate oven.

RICE CAKES.—Take eight yolks and four whites of eggs, and beat to a foam, add six ounces of powdered sugar, and the peel of one lemon grated; then stir in half a pound of ground rice, and beat all together for half an hour. Put it into a buttered tin, and bake twenty minutes. This cake is recommended as very easy of digestion. All the foregoing cakes are made without butter, and therefore are not apt to prove injurious.

RICE CAKES WITH BUTTER.—Beat, till extremely light, the yolks of nine eggs; add half a pound of sifted loaf sugar, and the same quantity of sifted rice flour; melt half a pound of fresh butter, and mix it with the eggs, sugar, and flour, along with a few pounded bitter almonds; half fill small buttered tins, and bake in a quick oven.

CURRANT CAKES.—Take half a pound of cleaned and dried currants, the same quantity of dried and sifted flour, a quarter of a pound of pounded sugar, a quarter of a pound of fresh butter, four yolks and three whites of eggs, both well beaten, and a little grated nutmeg or pounded cinna-mon; then beat the butter to a cream; add the sugar, and then the eggs and the flour; beat these well for twenty mi-nutes; mix in the currants and the grated nutmeg. Drop the cakes in a round form upon buttered paper, or bake them in small tins in a quick oven.

CARAWAY CAKES.—Take one pound of flour, half a pound of butter well rubbed into it, half a pound of sifted loaf su-gar, and half a teacup of caraway seeds; make them into a stiff paste with a little cold water, roll it out two or three times, cut it into round cakes, prick them, and bake them upon floured tins, in a slow oven. Currants may be used instead of caraway seeds, if preferred.

SUGAR CAKES.—Take half a pound of dried flour, a quarter of a pound of fresh butter, a quarter of a pound of sifted loaf sugar; then mix together the flour and the sugar; rub in the butter, and add the yolk of an egg beaten with a table-spoonful of cream; make it into a paste, roll, and cut it into small round cakes, which bake upon a floured tin.

TEA CAKES.—With a pound of flour rub a quarter of a pound of butter; add the beaten yolks of two, and the white of one egg, a quarter of a pound of pounded loaf sugar, and a few caraway seeds; mix it to a paste with a little warm milk, cover it with a cloth, and let it stand before the fire for nearly an hour; roll out the paste, and cut it into round cakes with the top of a glass, and bake them upon floured tins.

HARD GINGERBREAD.—Rub half a pound of butter into a pound of flour; then rub in half a pound of sugar, two table-spoonfuls of ginger, and a spoonful of rose water; work it well; roll out, and bake in flat pans in a moderate oven. It will take about half an hour to bake. This gingerbread will keep good some time.

SUGAR GINGERBREAD.—Take two pounds of flour, one pound of butter, and one of sugar, five eggs well beaten, two ounces of powdered ginger, and a tea-spoonful of pearlash.

COMMON GINGERBREAD.—Take a pound and a half of flour, and rub into it half a pound of butter; add half a pound of brown sugar and half a pint of molasses, two table-spoonfuls of cream, a tea-spoonful of pearlash, and ginger to the taste. Make it into a stiff paste, and roll it out thin. Put it on buttered tins, and bake in a moderate oven.

SOFT GINGERBREAD.—Six teacups of flour, three cups of molasses, three cups of cream, two of butter, one table-spoonful of pearlash, and the same of ginger. Bake in a quick oven about half an hour.

COMPOSITION CAKE.—Take one pound of flour, one pound of sugar, half a pound of butter, seven eggs, half a pint of cream, and spices to your taste. Beat all well together, and bake in a buttered tin, or in cups.

TUNBRIDGE CAKE.—Rub six ounces of butter into a quart of flour; then mix six ounces of sugar into three well-beaten eggs, and make the flour into paste, adding a little rose water and what spices you like. Roll the paste very thin, and cut with the top of a glass; prick the cakes with a fork, and cover with caraways, or wash with the white of an egg, and dust a little white sugar over. Bake on tins in a moderate oven.

COMMON PLUM CAKE.—Mix five ounces of butter with three pounds of dry flour and five ounces of fine-powdered sugar; add six ounces of currants, washed and dried, and some pimento or cinnamon and mace, finely powdered. Put three table-spoonfuls of good yeast into a pint of new milk warmed, and mix the dough; let it stand till it is light. Make it into twelve cakes, and bake on a floured tin half an hour. Raisins may be used instead of currants, if more convenient; but raisins must be stoned and chopped.

RICH PLUM OR WEDDING CAKE.—Take two pounds and a half of dried and sifted flour, allow the same quantity of fresh butter washed with rose water, two pounds of finely pounded loaf sugar, three pounds of cleaned and dried currants, one pound of raisins stoned, one nutmeg grated, half a pound of sweetmeats cut small, a quarter of a pound of blanched almonds pounded with a little rose water, and twenty eggs, the yolks and whites separately beaten. The butter must be beaten with the hand till it becomes like cream; then add the sugar, and by degrees the eggs; after these, the rest of the ingredients, mixing in at last the currants, with nearly a tea-cupful of rose or orange flower water. This mixture must be beaten together rather more than half an hour, then put into a cake-pan, which has previously been buttered and lined with buttered paper; fill it rather more than three quarters full. It should be baked in a moderate oven for three hours, and then cooled gradually, by at first letting it stand some time at the mouth of the oven.

If you fear the bottom of the cake may burn, put the pan on a plate with saw-dust between.

POUND CAKE.—Take one pound of dried and sifted flour, the same of loaf sugar and butter; the well-beaten yolks of twelve, and the whites of six eggs. Then with the hand beat the butter to a cream, add the sugar by degrees, then the eggs and the flour; beat it all well together for an hour, mixing half a glass of rose water, or twelve drops of the essence of lemon, and a nutmeg or a little cinnamon powdered. Bake it in a tin pan buttered, or in small ones in a quick oven.

PLUM POUND CAKE.—Take of dried and sifted flour, sifted loaf sugar, fresh butter, cleaned and dried currants, one pound each, and twelve eggs; then whisk the yolks and whites of the eggs separately, while another with the hand beats the butter to a cream; and as the froth rises upon the eggs, add it to the butter, and continue so doing till it is all beaten in; mix the flour and sugar together, and add them by degrees; the last thing, mix in the currants, together with a glass of rose water and a powdered nutmeg. It will require to be beaten during a whole hour. Bake it in a buttered tin.

HEART CAKES.—Beat one pound of butter to cream, with some rose water, one pound of flour dried, one pound of sifted sugar, twelve eggs; beat all well together; add a few currants washed and dried; butter small pans of a size for the purpose, heart-shaped; pour in the mixture; grate sugar over them: they are soon baked. They may be done in a Dutch oven.

FROST OR ICEING FOR CAKES.—Beat the whites of four eggs to a stiff foam, and add gradually three quarters of a pound of the best double-refined loaf sugar, pounded and sifted; mix in the juice of half a lemon, or a tea-spoonful of rose water. Beat the mixture till very light and white; place the cake before the fire, pour over the iceing, and smooth over the top and sides with the back of a spoon.

WARM CAKES FOR BREAKFAST AND TEA.—If I thought there was any hope of the advice being followed, I would say, do not eat any warm cakes at all; cold or toasted bread is far better for the constitution. But as most· people will have warm bread of some kind, a part of the time, at least, I consider it better to give directions for the sorts which seem likely to do the least injury; only adding here, that those persons will be *least* likely to be injured who eat the smallest quantity of hot cakes in proportion to their cold bread, which our customs allow.

TEA CAKES.—Rub into a pound of flour, two ounces of butter, a beaten egg, and half a tea-spoonful of salt; wet it with warmed milk; make the paste rather stiff, and let it remain before the fire, where it will be kept warm for an hour or two; then roll it thin, and cut it with the top of a tumbler; bake it quick.

BREAKFAST CAKE.—Put into a quart of flour four ounces of butter, and, if you use new milk, put in three large spoonfuls of yeast; make it into biscuits, and prick them with a fork.

If you have sour milk, omit the yeast, and put a tea-spoonful of pearlash in the sour milk; pour it while effervescing into the flour. These biscuits are less likely to injure the health, than if raised with yeast.

BUCKWHEAT CAKES.—Take one quart of buckwheat meal, a handful of Indian meal, and a tea-spoonful of salt; mix them with two large spoonfuls of yeast and sufficient cold water to make a thick batter. Put it in a warm place to rise, which will take three or four hours; or, if you mix it at night, let it stand where it is rather cool.

When it is light, bake it on a griddle, or in a pan. The griddle must be well buttered, and the cakes are better to be small and thin.

INDIAN SLAPJACKS.—Mix one pint of sifted Indian meal and four large spoonfuls of wheat flour into a quart of new milk, add four eggs beaten, and a little salt. Bake them on a griddle like buckwheat cakes; eat with butter and molasses.

PLAIN INDIAN CAKES.—Take a quart of sifted Indian meal, sprinkle a little salt over it, and mix it with scalding water, stirring it well; bake it on a board before the fire, or on a tin in a stove. It is healthy food for children, eaten warm (not *hot*) with molasses or milk.

Indian cake made with buttermilk, or sour milk, with a little cream or butter rubbed into the meal, and a tea-spoonful of pearlash in the milk, is very light and nutritious.

BATTER CAKES.—Beat two eggs, put them in half a pint of milk and a teacup of cream, with half a tea-spoonful of pearlash dissolved in it; sprinkle a tea-spoonful of salt, and grate half a nutmeg, a little cinnamon, and rose water, if you like. Stir in sifted flour till the batter is smooth and thick. Bake them on a griddle or in a pan. Butter the pan well, and drop the batter in small round cakes, and quite thin. They must be turned, nicely browned, but not made black; lay them on a plate, in a pile, with a little butter between each layer. This batter will make good pancakes, fried in hot lard.

CREAM SHORT CAKES.—In the country, where cream is plenty, this is a favorite cake at the tea table. Rub into a quart of flour a bit of butter as large as an egg, sprinkle over a tea-spoonful of salt; take half a pint of thick cream, a little sour, half a tea-spoonful of pearlash dissolved in water, poured into the cream, and milk added sufficient to wet the flour. Some use all cream, and that sweet. Then there needs no pearlash. It is expensive food.

ROLLS.—Rub into a pound of sifted flour two ounces of butter; beat the whites of three eggs to a froth and add a table-spoonful of good yeast, a little salt, and sufficient warm milk to make a stiff dough. Cover and put it where it will be kept warm, and it will rise in an hour. Then make it into rolls, or round cakes, put them on a floured tin, and bake in a quick oven or stove. They will be done in ten or fifteen minutes.

CHAPTER X.

CHEAP DISHES.

Not for the poor, but those who are growing rich—Indian bread—Puddings—Rice—Beef stewed—Mutton chops—Lamb fry—Veal liver—Veal and rice—An economical dinner—Hashes—Pea soup—Ox cheek soup—Fish—Cakes, Pies—Blackberry jam.

THIS chapter is *not* written for the *poor*. The two classes, which in our country constitute the poor, care little for economy. There is the miserable poor, usually made so by intemperance in drink; these seldom take any thought how they shall live, but cook whatever they can obtain in the readiest way; and there is the luxurious poor, who live on credit and by "speculations;" these are generally most fastidious in appetite and careless of expense; they would be disgusted at the thought of a "cheap dish." It is not for such that I shall take pains to prepare receipts for dishes combining the greatest economy of cost with the most nourishing and healthy materials—because it would be care and pains thrown away. But the rich, who intend to continue so, the thriving, who mean to be rich, the sensible and industrious, who love comfort and independence, the benevolent, who wish to do good—these classes all practise economy, and will not despise " cheap dishes."

CHEAP BREAD.—Indian meal is the cheapest, and a bushel furnishes more nutriment than the same quantity of wheat. It is also a generally healthy diet, and those who wish to practise close economy should use much of this meal in their families.

It makes excellent puddings, and warm cakes, which are much less apt to oppress the stomach than hot wheat bread or short cakes of any kind. And good, light, nourishing bread may be made by using five parts of Indian and one of rye or wheat flour, (see receipts for " Rye and Indian Bread;") which is better than to cook it hot at every meal.

Remember that *four* loaves of *cold bread* will go as far in a family as *five loaves of hot bread.*

PLAIN BAKED INDIAN PUDDING.—Scald a quart of skimmed milk, and stir in while it is hot, half a pint of sifted Indian meal add a tea-cup of molasses; season with a little salt, ginger, or cinnamon. Let it cool, (it is better to stand an hour or two,) then pour it into an earthen pot or deep pan, that has been well buttered, (clarified drippings will answer to rub the pan, but butter is best,) and bake it three or four hours. Pour in half a tea-cup of cold milk, and stir the whole when you set it in the oven.

INDIAN FRUIT PUDDING.—Take a pint of hot milk, and stir in Indian meal till the batter is stiff; add a tea-spoonful of salt and a little molasses; then stir in a pint of whortleberries, or the same quantity of chopped sweet apple. Tie it in a cloth that has been wet, and leave room for it to swell, or put it in a pudding pan, and tie a cloth over—boil it three hours. The water must boil when it is put in.

You can use cranberries, and eat it with sweet sauce.

HASTY PUDDING.—Boil water, a quart, three pints, or two quarts, according to the size of your family; sift your meal, stir five or six spoonfuls of it thoroughly into a bowl of water; when the water in the kettle boils, pour into it the contents of the bowl; stir it well, and let it boil up thick; put in salt to suit your own taste, then stand over the kettle, and sprinkle in meal, handful after handful, stirring it very thoroughly all the time, and letting it boil between whiles. When it is so thick that you stir it with great difficulty, it is about right. It takes half an hour's cooking. Eat it with milk or molasses. Either Indian meal or rye meal may be used. If the system is in a restricted state, nothing can be better than *rye* hasty pudding and *West India* molasses. This diet would save many a one the horrors of dyspepsia.

PLAIN BAKED RICE PUDDING.—A pint of rice, washed and boiled soft in a quart of milk with a salt-spoonful of salt; when cold, add three eggs, two cups of sugar, a small piece of butter, a little cinnamon or a nutmeg. Bake it an hour in a buttered dish.

PLAIN BOILED RICE.—Wash in four or five waters a pint of good rice; tie it in a pudding cloth, allowing plenty of room to swell; put it on in a pot of cold water, and let it boil slowly for two hours. It may be eaten with butter and sugar, or molasses.

PLAIN APPLE PUDDING.—Make a batter with two eggs, a pint of milk, and three or four spoonfuls of flour; pour it into a deep dish, and having pared six or eight small apples, place them whole in the batter, and bake it in a stove or oven. It will be done in an hour.

A CHEAP AND QUICK PUDDING.—Beat up four eggs, add a pint of milk and a little salt, and stir in four large spoonfuls of flour, a little nutmeg and sugar to your taste. Beat it well, and pour it into buttered teacups, filling them rather more than half full. They will bake in a stove or dutch oven in fifteen minutes; and if you have company to dinner, and wish to add a little dish, this is a good and cheap one.

BREAD PUDDING.—Pieces of dry bread, crust, &c., if kept clean, and used before they are sour, make good puddings; no prudent housekeeper will allow them to be wasted Soak the crusts in milk till they are soft; then add eggs, sweetening and spice to your taste. Bake or boil.

PEAS PUDDING.—Take a pint of good split peas, and having washed, soak them well in warm water; then tie them in a cloth, put the pudding into a sauce-pan of hot water, and boil it until quite soft. When done, beat it up with a little butter and salt; serve it with boiled pork or beef, or with a little cold meat it makes a good dinner for children in winter season.

PORK AND BEANS is an economical dish; but it does not agree with weak stomachs. Put a quart of beans into two quarts of cold water, and hang them all night over the fire, to swell. In the morning, pour off the water, rinse them well with two or three waters poured over them in a colander. Take a pound of pork that is not very fat, score the rind, then again place the beans just covered with water in the kettle, and keep them hot over the fire for an hour or two; then drain off the water, sprinkle a little pepper and a tea-spoonful of salt over the beans; place them in a well-glazed earthen pot, not very wide at the top, put the pork down in the beans, till the rind only appears; fill the pot with water till it just reaches the top of the beans, put it in a brisk oven, and bake three or four hours.

Stewed beans and pork are prepared in the same way, only they are kept over the fire, and the pork in them, three or four hours instead of being in the oven. The beans will not be white or pleasant to the taste unless they are well soaked and washed, nor are they healthy without this process.

BEEF STEAKS STEWED.—This is a very good and economical way of cooking steaks that are not very tender. Put the steaks in a stew-pan with a little butter, and fry them brown. · Then add a little gravy or boiling water, some pepper, salt, and a table-spoonful of vinegar, and let them stew gently till tender. Thicken the gravy with a bit of butter rolled in flour.

TO STEW A ROUND OF BEEF.—Tie up the beef with a strong tape, and put it on to stew with as much cold water as will cover it—season with salt, black pepper, a little all-spice, mace or cloves, and a gill of vinegar. Let it stew gently, skimming it well, seven or eight hours, till it is tender. Take out the beef, skim off the fat, strain the gravy, and thicken with a little flour, let it boil, and pour it over the beef before serving.

This is a rich dish, and economical, because stewing meat saves all the juices and essence.

BAKED MUTTON CHOPS.—Cut a neck of mutton into neat chops, season them with salt and pepper, butter a dish, lay in the chops, and pour over them a batter made of a quart of milk, four eggs beaten up, four table-spoonfuls of flour, and a little salt. An hour will bake them. This is a quick mode of dressing a dinner, if you are baking.

LAMB FRY.—Take the heart, liver, and sweet bread of a lamb; cut it into slices, and fry it in salt pork fat, or dip it in the beaten white of an egg, and strew bread crumbs over it, before you fry it. Garnish with crisp parsley.

VEAL LIVER.—There is none of the solid meat of animals so cheap as the liver, and, if well cooked, it makes a good dish. Cut it in thin slices, rub them with flour or Indian meal, and fry in salt pork fat till thoroughly done; or you may broil it like steak. Beef liver is cooked in the same way.

VEAL AND RICE.—Take one pound of veal; wash the same quantity of rice, and stew them together in three quarts of water, seasoned with pepper and salt. Let it stew gently two hours, then add half a pint of milk, and let it just come to a simmer. This with boiled potatoes will make a comfortable dinner for a large family.

A VERY ECONOMICAL DINNER.—One pound of sausages cut in pieces, with four pounds of potatoes, and a few onions, if they are liked, with about a table-spoonful of flour mixed in a pint of water and added to the dish, will make a sufficient dinner for five or six persons. The potatoes must be cut in slices, and stewed with the sausages till tender.

Or you may use a pound and a half of meat (mutton is best) instead of the sausages. Season with pepper, salt and sage or thyme.

HASHES.—All the pieces and bits of cold meat should be minced and warmed; if this is rightly done, the dish is generally a favorite one.

It is best to chop the meat very fine, (gristles and gelatinous matter from the bones may be included;) then make a gravy by putting a lump of butter (what you judge necessary) into a stew-pan; when it is hot, add a little flour, and stir it into the butter; then add a teacupful of the broth the meat was boiled in, and a little catsup. Let this boil up, then put in the mince meat, with a little chopped parsley, pepper and salt. Let it stand and simmer a few minutes covered, but do not let it boil—it hardens the meat to boil it. Lay slices of toasted bread in the dish, and pour the meat and gravy over.

PEA SOUP WITHOUT MEAT.—Take a quart of green peas, keep out half a pint of the youngest; boil them separately, and put them in the soup when it is finished;) put them on in boiling water; boil them tender, and then pour off the water, and set it by to make the soup with; put the peas into a mortar, and pound them into a mash; then put them into two quarts of the water you boiled the peas in; stir all well together; let it boil up for about five minutes, and then rub it through a hair sieve. If the peas are good, it will be as thick and fine a vegetable soup as need be sent to table.

OX CHEEK SOUP.—Separate the bones from the meat, break the former, cut the meat into pieces the length of a finger and the breadth of two, put a quart of water to every pound of meat, with a little salt, set it on a gentle fire, and skim it well during the first boiling; after it has stewed gently two hours, add carrots, turnips, onions, celery, a head of cabbage, and a bunch of sweet herbs, pepper, salt, and a quarter of a pound of vermicelli; let it stew two hours and a half longer, skim it, and take out the herbs and bones. Rice may be used instead of vermicelli, and potatoes instead of cabbage. This is an economical dinner for a number of laboring men.

A STEW SOUP.—Take half a pound of beef, mutton or pork, cut it in small pieces, and put it into seven pints of water; add half a pint of dry peas or rice, two turnips and ten potatoes, all cut small, and two onions. Let the whole stew gently for about three hours. Season with pepper and salt, and thicken with a little flour, if needed.

Salt Meat Stew may be made in the same manner, only put the meat in about an hour before adding the vegetables. A cabbage head cut up and put into these stews makes them rich and savory.

To stew Meat is the most economical way in which it can be cooked.

Fish.—The salted cod fish is cheap food, if potatoes are used freely with it. Thick fish are more profitable than thin ones. To cook salt fish well, requires considerable care. It should never *boil;* put it on in cold water, and let it soak over night. Then wash and scrape it very clean; put it into a kettle of warm water, and let it stand near the fire where it can be hot, but not boil up, for two hours. It should be scalding hot the last half hour. Drain it, and send it to table. Egg sauce or melted butter is eaten with it.

Should any fish remain after dinner, have it minced before it is put away, and the potatoes mashed up with it. They can be done much better and easier when warm than if allowed to stand till morning. Then the fish may be rolled into balls, flattened and fried in hot butter or lard. Dip the balls into the beaten white of an egg, and they will not break. This is a good dish for breakfast in the winter season.

Cakes, Pies, etc.—In making these kinds of food, people who live in the country must often use maple or brown sugar; in these cases, always dry it well for cake, or pound it fine.

Honey or molasses will answer for preserves of fruit that are to be used in the family; but they will not keep unless scalded often.

Blackberry Jam.—Gather the fruit in dry weather; allow half a pound of coarse brown sugar to every pound of fruit; boil the whole together gently for an hour, or till the blackberries are soft, stirring and mashing them well. Preserve it like any other jam, and it will be found very useful in families, particularly for children, regulating their bowels, and enabling you to dispense with cathartics. It may be spread on bread or on puddings instead of butter; and even when the blackberries are bought, it is cheaper than butter. In the country, every family should preserve, at least, a half a peck of blackberries.

CHAPTER XI.

DRINKS.

Remarks on family drinks—-Coffee—-Shells—-Chocolate—Tea—- Common Beer—Spruce—Ginger—Lemonade— Orangeade—Currant Wine—Water.

THERE is one rule for drinks which no *woman* should violate—never make any preparation of which *alcohol* forms a part for family use!

Let distilled liquors, of every name and sort, be religiously banished from that sanctuary of domestic comfort, *our homes*, and the appetite for them would, in a great degree, become extinguished. And if we rightly feel the importance of guarding our own families from the insidious destroyer, can we be guilty of the *in*hospitality of pressing on our friends the poison, which, however it may be disguised by delicious flavors, is still the same in character, the deadly foe of social improvement and human happiness!

Leaving the preparations of alcohol out of our account, the other mixtures for family drinks which require receipts, are few and simple. The one which demands most care and consideration is coffee. That this beverage is rarely made right in our country, all who have drank it in France or the East, affirm; and whether the bad effects it not unfrequently produces on the health of those who use it freely, arise from this defect in preparation, or from our climate, or the nature of coffee itself, has never been satisfactorily settled. It certainly does in America often prove injurious to those who drink it very strong; and therefore it is best to use it cautiously : those who are at all inclined to be dyspeptic or nervous, should abstain altogether.

There are several methods of making coffee, each highly recommended—I cannot decide which is best, but the following way is a good one :—

To MAKE COFFEE.—Take fresh-roasted coffee, (a quarter of a pound for three persons is the rule, but *less* will do ;) allow two table-spoonfuls for each person, grind it just before making, put it in a basin and break into it an egg, yolk, white, shell and all. Mix it up with the spoon to the consistence of mortar, put in a warm not *boiling* water in the coffee pot ; let it boil up and *break* three times ; then stand a few minutes, and it will be as clear as amber, and the egg will give it a rich taste.

ANOTHER WAY TO MAKE COFFEE.—Pour hot water into your coffee pot, and then stir in your coffee, a spoonful at a time, allowing three to every pint of water ; this makes *strong* coffee. Stir it to prevent the mixture from boiling over, as the coffee swells, and to force it to combine with the water. This will be done after it has boiled gently a few minutes. Then let it stand and boil slowly for half an hour ; remove it from the fire, and pour in a tea-cup of cold water, and set it in the corner to settle. As soon as it becomes clear, it is to be poured, gently, into a clean coffee pot for the table.

Made in this manner it may be kept two or three days in summer, and a week in winter ; you need only heat it over when wanted.

The grounds and sediment may be boiled over and used once for coffee.

Fish skin is often used to settle coffee, and will answer tolerably well, if rightly prepared. Pull off the skin from a salted cod ; scrape, wash and dry it in the oven, after removing the bread ; then divide it in pieces about an inch square, and put it in a paper bag for use. It will require one bit for every pint of water ; put in when you make the coffee. Several substitutes for coffee are used by those who cannot afford the real berry—rye, peas, &c. None of these are very healthy, and certainly are not good. The best substitute is toasted crust of bread, but it is cheaper to drink water, and if taken for a little time will be as palatable ; or else use

Cocoa Shells.—These should be soaked over night, then boil them in the same water in the morning. They are considerably nutritious, allowed to be healthy, and are cheap.

Chocolate.—To each square of chocolate, scraped off fine, and put in the pot, allow a pint (less if you like it strong) of water. Stir it while boiling; and let it be uncovered. Let it boil about fifteen minutes, or half an hour, then pour in your cream or rich milk, and let it boil up. Nutmeg grated over a cup of chocolate improves the flavor.

Tea.—Scald the teapot with boiling water; then put in the tea, allowing three tea-spoonfuls to a pint of water—or for every two persons. Pour on the water. It must be boiling hot, and let the tea steep about ten minutes.

Black tea is healthier than green. Hyson and Souchong mixed together, half and half, is a pleasanter beverage than either alone, and safer for those who drink *strong* tea, than to trust themselves wholly with green.

Common Beer.—Two gallons of water to a large handful of hops is the rule. A little fresh-gathered spruce or sweet fern makes the beer more agreeable, and you may allow a quart of wheat bran to the mixture; then boil it two or three hours. Strain it through a sieve, and stir in, while the liquor is hot, a teacup of molasses to every gallon. Let it stand till lukewarm, pour it into a clean barrel and add good yeast, a pint, if the barrel is nearly full; shake it well together; it will be fit for use the next day.

Spruce Beer.—Allow an ounce of hops and a spoonful of ginger to a gallon of water. When well boiled, strain it, and put in a pint of molasses and half an ounce or less of the essence of spruce; when cool, add a teacup of yeast, and put into a clean tight cask, and let it ferment for a day or two, then bottle it for use. You can boil the sprigs of spruce fir in room of the essence.

Ginger Beer quickly made.—A gallon of boiling water is poured over three quarters of a pound of loaf sugar, one ounce of ginger, and the peel of one lemon; when milk-warm, the juice of the lemon and a spoonful of yeast are added. It should be made in the evening, and bottled next morning, in stone bottles, and the cork tied down with twine.

Good brown sugar will answer, and the lemon may be omitted, if *cheapness* is required.

LEMONADE.—Three lemons to a pint of water, makes strong lemonade; sweeten to your taste.

This is the best beverage for social parties; cool, refreshing, pleasant, and salubrious.

ORANGEADE.—Roll and press the juice from the oranges in the same way as from lemons. It requires less sugar than lemonade. The water must be pure and cold, and then there can be nothing more delicious than these two kinds of drink.

CURRANT WINE.—Gather the currants when dry, extract the juice, either by mashing and pressing the fruit, or putting it in a jar, placed in boiling water; strain the juice, and for every gallon allow one gallon of water and three pounds of sugar. Dissolve the sugar in the water, and take off the scum; let it cool, add it to the currant juice, and put the mixture in a keg, but do not close it tightly till it has ceased fermenting, which will not be under a week. In three or four weeks it may be bottled. The white of an egg beaten, mixed with a tea-spoonful of cream of tartar, and stirred into the liquid, makes the wine look clear and bright.

EAU SUCRE.—Sweeten boiling water with sugar to your taste. This beverage is much used by French ladies. It is considered soporific, and good for fatigued or weak nerves.

WATER.—The foregoing receipts will teach the manner of preparing those drinks which are most agreeable to the palate, suitable for the purposes of hospitality, economy, and that attention to the real welfare of a family, which should never be neglected.

But after all, the best beverage for the healthy, who wish to continue well, is good pure cold water! The danger in recommending it as the common and constant drink for all persons, at all times and places, arises from the difficulty of finding it pure and good. There is no doubt that, besides the diseases known to be generated by drinking bad water, serious injury is frequently inflicted on the constitution from the long-continued use of much that is called *good;* that is, though known to be *hard*, and consequently impregnated with chemical solutions of lime, still it does not taste unpleasant, and is clear.   But this *hard* water always leaves a mineral matter on the skin, when we use it in washing, which renders the hands and face rough and liable to chap. Does not this water, if we drink it, likewise corrode and injure the fine membranes of the stomach? The Boston people, who constantly use hard water for all purposes of cookery and drink, certainly have bad complexions, sallow, dry, and *hard*-looking; and complaints of the stomach or dyspepsia are very common among them.*

A Salem gentleman declared, that when his daughters, who frequently visited at Boston, passed two or three weeks at a time there, he could see a very material change in their complexions.   At Salem there is plenty of soft water, and the ladies of that ancient town are famed for their beauty, which is chiefly owing (its superiority I mean) to a peculiarly fair, delicate tincture of skin, contrasted with the half-petrified appearance of those who are obliged to drink *hard water* always, and often to wash in it.

The best water to drink as well as wash with, when it can be obtained pure, or rendered so, is *rain-water*.   This may generally be effected with a little care and expense. A clean reservoir to collect the rain water is needed, and a portable filterer—that is all the expense; the care of filtering, every young lady who values her health or *complexion*, always synonymous, will gladly undertake.

Filtering cools the water, and in the summer ice may be used.

CHEAP SUBSTITUTE FOR A WATER FILTER.—Lay a thick bed of pounded charcoal at the bottom of a large common earthen flower-pot; over this lay a bed of fine sand, about four inches thick.

A bit of quick-lime thrown into a water-cask is useful in purifying the water.   Agitating the water and exposing

---

* It has been computed that the Boston people have drank sufficient lime, were it collected together, to build the Bunker Hill Monument as high as it was ever designed to be carried—190 feet.

it to the air, will both soften it and help to keep it fresh. Strain muddy water through a fine sieve in which a cloth and sponge, or layer of fine sand, or charcoal, is placed.

CHAPTER XII.

HOUSEHOLD ECONOMY.

IF you would practise this economy to the greatest advantage, be regular in the arrangement of your work, punctual in preparing your meals, and take good care that *nothing is wasted.*

It is best to have the washing done on Mondays, if this can be managed without encroaching on that rest from labor, which the holy Sabbath should always bring, as well to the domestics as to every other member of a Christian family. But whether Monday or Tuesday be the day, let it be fixed, and the washing never omitted when it is *possible* to have it done. The next morning, *early*, should be the time to begin ironing, so that the clothes may have time to be aired and put away before night.

Mend clothes *before* washing, except stockings; these can best be darned when clean.

FLANNELS should be washed in clean hot suds in which a little bluing has been mingled; do not rinse them. Woollens of all kinds should be washed in hot suds.

SOFT WATER is indispensable to the washerwoman; rain, or river water, is the best. If you have good water, do not use soda; it gives a yellowish tinge to the clothes. If you buy your soap, it is most economical to use hard soap for washing clothes, and soft soap for floors, &c.

COLORED DRESSES.—Turn the inner side out, and wash them in cold water, in which a little boiled soap is well mixed; rinse them well in cléan cold water, and the last time with a little salt in the water, and dry them in the shade. They should be washed and dried with as much expedition as possible.

MILDEW STAINS are very difficult to remove from linen. The most effectual way is to rub soap on the spots, then chalk, and bleach the garment in the hot sun.

INK AND IRON MOULD may be taken out by wetting the spots in milk, then covering them with common salt. It should be done before the garments have been washed. Another way to take out ink is to dip it in melted tallow. For fine, delicate articles, this is the best way.

FRUIT AND WINE STAINS.—Mix two tea-spoonfuls of water and one of spirit of salt, and let the stained part lie in this for two minutes; then rinse in cold water. Or wet the stain with hartshorn.

TO WASH CARPETS.—Shake and beat it well; lay it upon the floor, and tack it firmly; then with a clean flannel wash it over with one quart of bullock's gall, mixed with three quarts of soft cold water, and rub it off with a clean flannel or house cloth. Any particular dirty spot shuld be rubbed with pure gall.

TO CLEAN PAINT.—Put a very little pearlash, or soda, in the water to soften it, then wash the paint with flannel and soft soap; wash the soap off, and wipe dry with a clean linen cloth.

TO CLEAN PAPER WALLS.—The very best method is to sweep off lightly all the dust, then rub the paper with stale bread—cut the crust off very thick, and wipe straight down from the top, then begin at the top again, and so on.

CARPETS.—The oftener these are taken up and shaken, the longer they will wear, as the dust and dirt underneath grind them out. Sweep carpets with a stiff hair brush, instead of *an old corn broom*, if you wish them to wear long or look well. At any rate, keep a good *broom purposely* for the carpet.

TO POLISH MAHOGANY FURNITURE.—Rub it with *cold drawn linseed oil*, and polish by rubbing with a clean dry cloth, after wiping the oil from the furniture. Do this once a week, and your mahogany tables will be so finely polished that hot water would not injure them. The reason is this, linseed oil hardens when exposed to the air; and when it has filled all the pores of the wood, the surface becomes hard, and smooth like glass.

To TAKE INK OUT OF MAHOGANY.—Mix in a tea-spoonful of cold water, a few drops of oil of vitriol; touch the spot with a feather dipped in the liquid.

To CLEAN PICTURES.—Dust them lightly with cotton wool, or with a feather brush.

To CLEAN MIRRORS.—Wipe them lightly with a clean bit of sponge or fine linen that has been wet in spirits of wine, or in soft water; then dust the glass with fine whiting powder; rub this off with a soft cloth—then rub with another clean cloth, and finish it with a silk handkerchief. Dust the frames with cotton wool.

To CLEAN STRAW CARPETS.—Wash them in salt and water, and wipe them with a clean dry cloth.

To CLEAN MARBLE.—Pound very finely a quarter of a pound of whiting and a small quantity of stone blue; dissolve in a little water one ounce of soda, and mix the above ingredients carefully together with a quarter of a pound of soft soap; boil it a quarter of an hour on a slow fire, carefully stirring it. Then, when quite hot, lay it with a brush upon the marble, and let it remain on half an hour. Wash it off with warm water, flannel, and a scrubbing brush, and wipe it dry.

To CLEAN FREESTONE.—Wash the hearth with soap, and wipe it with a wet cloth. Or rub it over with a little freestone powder, after washing the hearth in hot water. Brush off the powder when dry.

To BLACK A BRICK HEARTH.—Mix some black lead with soft soap and a little water, and boil it—then lay it on with a brush. Or mix the lead with water only.

To CLEAN BRASS.—Rub it over with a bit of flannel dipped in sweet oil—then rub it hard with finely powdered rotten stone—then rub it with a soft linen cloth—and polish with a bit of wash leather.

Rub *creaking hinges* with soft soap.

GLASSES should be washed and rinsed in cold water, and the water wiped off with one cloth; then rub dry and clean with another.

CUT GLASS should be rubbed with a damp sponge dipped in whiting, then brush this off with a clean brush, and wash the vessel in cold water.

An ironing board, sheets, and holders, should always be kept purposely for the ironing.   A small board—two feet by fourteen inches wide, covered with old flannel and then with fine cotton, is handy to iron small articles on.

ISINGLASS is a most delicate starch for fine muslins. When boiling common starch, sprinkle in a little fine salt; it will prevent its sticking.

BED LINEN should be well aired before it is used.   Keep your sheets folded in pairs on a shelf—closets are better than drawers or chests for linen, it will not be so likely to gather damp.

HAIR, *or even straw mattresses,* are more healthy to sleep on than feather beds.   Never put children on these heating beds.   Keep your sleeping rooms very clean and well aired; and do not cumber them with unnecessary furniture.

BED CURTAINS are unhealthy, because they confine the air around us while we are asleep.

When baking is done twice a week, Wednesdays and Saturdays should be chosen; if only once a week, Saturday is the best, because it allows of preparation for the Sunday dinner—a pudding can be baked—and meat, too, if the family have a *real* desire of keeping the day for that which it was evidently intended, rest from worldly care, as well as for moral and religious improvement.

OLD BREAD may be made almost as good as new by putting it in the oven after the bread is drawn, or in a stove, and let it heat through.

CRUSTS and pieces of bread should be kept in an earthen pot or pan, closely covered in a dry cool place.

Keep fresh lard and suet in tin vessels.

Keep salt pork fat in glazed earthen ware.

Keep yeast in wood or earthen.

Keep preserves and jellies in glass, china, or stone ware.

Keep salt in a dry place.

Keep meal in a cool, dry place.

Keep ice in the cellar, wrapped in flannel.

Keep vinegar in wood or glass.

Housekeepers in the country must be careful that their meats are well salted, and kept under brine.

Sugar is an admirable ingredient in curing meat, butter and fish.

Saltpetre dries up meat—it is best to use it sparingly.

To PRESERVE EGGS.—Cover the bottom of a small tub or cask with coarse salt—then place a layer of fresh eggs, standing *upright* on the large end—cover these with salt—then put another layer of eggs; and so on, till the tub is full. Keep it in a cool, dry place, and the eggs will remain good for a year. The last layer should be of *salt*, and an inch in thickness.

In the summer season, when eggs are not put in salt, they should be *turned* every day. Rubbing them over with butter or oil is said to make them keep fresh for several weeks.

Always break eggs for cake, &c., into a tea-cup, one by one, before putting them into the basin to be beaten. Then the bad ones can be easily detected.

THE DAIRY.—Always to make *good* butter or cheese shows great care and excellent judgment in the farmer's wife. When every department of the dairy is kept perfectly neat, there is hardly any exhibition of woman's industry more likely to make her husband proud, or gratify a beholder of good sense and benevolence, than the sight of a neat dairy-room filled with the rich, valuable productions which her skill has fashioned from the milk of the cow.

"The farmer's wife," says the accomplished Addison, "who has made nine hundred cheeses, and brought up half a dozen healthy children, is far more *amiable* in the eyes of unprejudiced reason, than the fine lady, who has made two millions of insipid visits, and propagated scandal from one end of the town to the other." The moral of this sentiment is true; rational employment, the industry either of hand or head, which produces benefit to society, is the real test of excellence in character,—and few American ladies desire any other standard.

The secret of success in the dairy is strict attention and scrupulous neatness in all its operations. The best time to make butter is in June, when the pastures are rich with clover, and September, when the *fall* feed is in its perfection. July and August are the months for cheese; then the rich new milk and cream cheeses are made.

Dairy work must be learned by practice, and requires as nice judgment and taste as cake-making. A few general directions may be followed to advantage ; but there have not yet been any settled rules for this work which will insure good butter and cheese ; it seems to depend very much on the skill of the individual manager, who does not often choose to communicate the secret of her infallible success. It is to be hoped that some of the intelligent women who are eminently successful in managing the dairy, will give the result of their experience—we might then frame receipts which would be very advantageous to the young farmer's wife, and of great benefit to the public ; for it is a real calamity to have poor butter and cheese sent to market.   Bad butter, particularly, is not only unhealthy, but it entirely spoils every good article of food in which it is mingled. Never purchase it, let it be ever so cheap.   It is far better to eat molasses, or honey, or preserves, with bread, and use lard, beef drippings, suet, &c. for gravies and shortening, than to use bad butter.

To insure good butter, you must always scald your pans, pails, &c. in hot water, and then heat them by the fire, or in the hot sun, so that they may be perfectly sweet.

Keep your cream in a cool place in the summer, and churn twice a week.

Work out all the butter-milk.—This must be done, or the butter will not keep well; and do not make the butter too salt.

Never put butter in a pine tub.

Pickle for Butter.—Allow half a pound of salt, an ounce of saltpetre, and half a pound of sugar to three quarts of water.—Dissolve them together ; scald and skim the pickle; let it be entirely cold, and then pour it over the butter.

Keep your cheese in a dark, cool room, and turn and rub them every day.   The fat fried out of salt pork, is the best preservative to rub on cheese, and gives a rich color and smoothness to the rind.

Never wash your cheese shelves; but always wipe them clean with a dry cloth, when you turn your cheese.

Do not heat the milk too hot; it should never, for new milk cheese, be more than blood warm; be sure that your rennet is good, and do not use more than it requires to bring the curd.

Cover the pan or tub in which milk is set to coagulate, and do not disturb it for half an hour or more.

Cut the curd, when fully formed, carefully with a knife; never break it with your hand; and be very particular, when draining it from the whey, not to squeeze or handle the curd; if you make the *white whey* run from the curd, you lose much of the richness of the cheese.

TO CURE BUTTER IN THE BEST MANNER.—The following receipt is from " The Housewife's Manual," a work said to have been prepared by *Sir Walter Scott.*

Having washed and beaten the butter free of buttermilk, work it quickly up, allowing a scanty half ounce of fine salt to the pound. Let the butter lie for twenty-four hours, or more; then, for every pound, allow a half ounce of the following mixture :—Take four ounces of salt, two of loaf-sugar, and a quarter of an ounce of saltpetre. Beat them all well together, and work the mixture thoroughly into the butter; then pack it down in jars or tubs. Instead of strewing a layer of salt on the top of the butter, which makes the first slice unfit for use, place a layer of the above mixture in folds of thin muslin, stitch it loosely, and lay this neatly over the top, which will effectually preserve it.

To freshen salt butter.—Churn it anew in sweet milk, a quart to the pound. The butter will gain in weight.

To improve rancid butter.—Wash it, melt it gradually, skim it, and put to it a slice of charred or hard-toasted bread, or some bits of charcoal.

CHAPTER XIII.

HINTS TO HELP.

" A rolling stone gathers no moss."
" Honesty is the best policy."
" A still tongue makes a wise head."—*Old Proverbs.*

DOMESTICS in American families are very differently situated from persons of the same class in any other part of the world. Few enter the employment with any intention of remaining servants; it is only for a present resource to obtain a living and a little cash, so that they may begin business or house-keeping for themselves.

American *help*, therefore, should be very particular in their good behavior, and be careful to do by their employers as they will want *help* to do by them, when their turn to keep domestics shall arrive.

Never leave a good place because a little fault has been found with your work . it is a very great injury to a domestic to change her place often; she will soon have the name of being bad tempered, and besides, she cannot gain friends : you must remain some time in a family before they will become attached to you. And if you are, as is generally the case, out of employment for a week before you go to a new place, you lose your time; and often have to pay for board too ; thus a loss of two or three weeks' wages is incurred; because you will not bear to be reproved, even for a fault. What folly ! thus to punish yourself for the sake of punishing your mistress, even if she did blame you without cause. The better way is to remain and behave so well that she shall be made to acknowledge your excellence ; which she will be pretty sure to do, if she finds you faithfully try to please her.

Do not think it degrades you to endeavor to please your employer. It surely adds to your respectability, for it shows that you live with people you respect. You are bound to please your employers as far as you honestly can, while you receive your wages. No person hires a domestic to be idle, cross, or disrespectful. It is worse than theft to take wages from your employers which you must know you have not earned, if you have been unfaithful, impertinent, and quarrelsome, and made them constant trouble.

Resolve, therefore, when you go as *help*, to prove *help* indeed, which you will be if you practise the following rules :

Always treat and speak of your employers with respect.

Be faithful and honest in managing all that they entrust to you.

Be kind and obliging to every body, particularly to all the domestics of the family.

In a word—do to others, in all things, as you would wish them to do by you in similar circumstances.

If you conduct thus, you will, though working in the kitchen, be as really respectable and independent as the lady in the parlor. In truth, she will be more dependent on your assistance than you will be on her for employment, and she will feel this, and treat you with the consideration and kindness which your merit deserves. But do not presume on this favor, and grow slack and careless. As long as you find it necessary to receive wages, be conscientious to perform all your duties as help.

Never think any part of your business too trifling to be well done.

The foregoing are general rules ; a few particular directions may be needed.

One of the faults which a cook should most seriously guard against, is bad temper. She has a good many trials. Her employment, in the summer season, is not a pleasant or healthy one—obliged as she is, to be over the hot fire, and confined, often, in a dark, close kitchen. Then she sometimes has a difficult lady to please, who does not know when the work is done well, and often gives contradictory or impracticable orders.

And the other domestics frequently interrupt the arrangements of the cook ; or, she is not furnished with proper implements and articles. All these things try her patience, and if it *sometimes* fails, we ought not too much to blame her. But she need not be always *cross*. And she should remember, too, her privileges—mistress of the kitchen, the highest wages, and, if she conducts well, the favorite always of her employers.

It is in the power of the cook to do much for the comfort and prosperity of the family ; if she is economical and conducts with propriety, the whole establishment goes on pleasantly ; but if she is cross, *intemperate*, and wasteful, the mischief and discomfort she causes are very great.   Never let the family have reason to say—" The cook is always cross !"

Intemperance is said to be the failing of cooks, oftener than of other domestics.   It is a vice which, if persisted in, will soon destroy the character and usefulness of the best cook.   Every one who desires to sustain a respectable station in her employment, must abstain *totally* from spirituous liquors.   " Touch not, taste not, handle not."   It is poison to your blood ; it is death to your reputation, if not to your body and soul.

Country girls who come to the cities as help, because they can there obtain large wages, should be careful in their diet.   Remember that as you cannot take so much exercise in the open air, you must live sparingly at first, or the change will injure your health.   And all that injures the health, injures also the bloom and beauty of youth.

To take a young woman, one of our farmer's daughters, from the free, pure air of the country, and confine her in the hot kitchen, often under ground, of one of our crowded city establishments, is such a change, that unless she is very particular in her care of herself, will soon cause her to look old, haggard, and disagreeable.   Her hair will be often matted with sweat and dust, and her complexion like a mummy. To avoid these unpleasant results, let the cook, from the first, adopt the following rules :—

1st. Eat regular meals, instead of tasting of every good thing you cook, till you have no appetite for food.

2d. Keep your sleeping room well aired, and your skin clean.

The best way is to wash yourself thoroughly when going to bed ; comb your hair also, and wear a night-cap or handkerchief on your head.   The next morning, you will only require to smooth your hair, not take it down, and wash your face and hands. It would look neater, and keep your hair much smoother, if you would wear a cap or handkerchief while at work, as English servants do.

Let your dress be of good, durable materials, that will wash well; keep it clean as possible, and always wear an apron.

In the afternoon, when the work is done, then you can wash and dress as neatly as you choose, only remember that a domestic in a showy, flimsy gown, and decked out with pinchbeck rings and ear ornaments, always makes a ridiculous figure in the eyes of every sensible person; because such persons see that you are spending your hard-earned wages for that which really does you no good.

Keep your kitchen, and all the utensils, clean and neat as possible. Sweep the chimney often, with an old broom kept for the purpose, so that no soot may collect to fall down on the dishes at the fire, and be sure that the hearth is neat as a table.

Always have plenty of hot water ready; and take care that your wiping cloths are washed every day.

The three rules you must follow, if you would always have your work done well, are these :—

"Do every thing at the proper time.

Keep every thing in its proper place.

Use every thing for its proper purpose."

If your mistress professes to understand cookery, the best way will be to follow her directions; if you find the dish is not so good as when cooked in your own way, respectfully ask her to let you try once alone. But never be angry or pout when you are told how your employer wishes to have the work done.

The great fault of the Irish *help* is, that they undertake to do what they have never learned. They will not acknowledge their ignorance; if they would do this, and patiently try to learn, they would soon, with their natural quickness, become good cooks—if they have good teachers. And what a privilege and blessing it is to a poor Irish girl, who has only lived in a hovel, with scarcely an article of furniture, save the pot "to boil the praties," to be instructed in household work! It is really a fortune to her; she can then always have good places and good pay, and soon clothe herself well, and lay up money.

There are benevolent and sensible ladies who do act thus kindly by the Irish girl; not only learn her how to work in the kitchen, but teach her needlework, and instruct her in reading and writing.

If you have had such a kind mistress, my poor girl, for the honor of old Ireland be grateful and faithful to your benefactress; and show yourself worthy to be the mother of American citizens; for to such good fortune your children, should you marry, will be entitled.

There is no danger that our domestics will have too much ambition, if it be of the right kind—the ambition of doing their duty as faithful, capable *help*, while they continue to work for others. But I would wish every young female domestic to *hope* that she may some time be mistress of her *own house;* and I would urge her to improve every opportunity she has of learning the best and most prudent manner of doing all kinds of work. Then she will be fitted to make her husband happy, and bring up her children to be respectable members of society.

One of the most certain evidences that she is worthy to enjoy prosperity, is her faithfulness to promote the interest of those for whom she works. If she is really trustworthy, she will show it in her conduct.

There is a class of cooks who cannot be trusted; every thing they dare take is slyly carried out of the house, and given to their friends; and they go on with this system of pilfering till they are turned away from every respectable place.

Do not be tempted to begin this system, nor think that the broken bits, which the family may not need, belong to you. The mistress of the house must manage these charities; ask her, and if she give you leave to dispose of the broken pieces, be very careful not to *make fragments* unnecessarily for the sake of giving them to your poor relations.

Act, in all these things, as you would if your employer was looking on you; and forget not that One, to whom you are more responsible than to any earthly master or mistress, is constantly watching you.

CHAPTER XIV.

HINTS TO HOUSEKEEPERS.

"It is much the same in governments as in families ; those states-men and housewives, who make a great bustle about the difficulties they are in, are the very ones who are too indolent, too awkward, or too ignorant to remove them."—MADAME ROLAND.

THE term *housekeeper*, in this book, is used in its Ameri-can signification, the same as " Mistress of the family," or " Lady of the house."

In our republican land, thanks to its rational institutions, which preserve in a high degree of purity the moral relations of domestic life, it is rare to find a married woman who does not superintend personally, the economy of her own household, let the wealth, profession, or political station of her husband be what it may. The most delicate lady, un-less her ill health were the pretext, would scarcely boast of retaining a hired housekeeper to perform her duties; and no lady would gain credit or consequence in society by so doing. In truth, our richest and most fashionable women are often models of good housekeeping ; many whose talents and accomplishments would adorn the first circles of Eu-rope, perform the woman's part of superintending the affairs of their own household, as scrupulously and well as though they had been taught nothing besides.

That the American ladies are better educated in all the solid branches of learning, than those of any other country in the world, there is no doubt—even Englishmen acknow-ledge their superior intelligence—and their good housekeep-ing proves the assertion of Miss Sedgwick true, namely, that the more intelligent a woman becomes, other things being equal, the more judiciously she will manage her domestic concerns. And we may add, that the more real knowledge she possesses of the great principles of morals, philosophy and human happiness, the more importance she will attach to her station, and the name of a " good housekeeper." It it is only the frivolous, and those who are superficially taught,

or only instructed in showy accomplishments, who despise
and neglect the ordinary duties of life as beneath their notice.   Such persons have not sufficient clearness of reason
to see that " Domestic Economy" includes every thing which
is calculated to make people love home and feel happy there.

One of the first duties of woman in domestic life is to
understand the quality of provisions and the preparation of
wholesome food.

The powers of the mind, as well as those of the body, are
greatly dependent on what we eat and drink.   The stomach
must be in health, or the brain cannot act with its utmost
vigor and clearness, nor can there be strength of muscle to
perform the purposes of the will.

But further, woman, to be qualified for the duty which
Nature has assigned her, that of promoting the health, happiness and improvement of her species, must understand
the natural laws of the human constitution, and the causes
which often render the efforts she makes to please the appetite of those she loves, the greatest injury which could be
inflicted upon them.   Often has the affectionate wife caused
her husband a sleepless night and severe distress, which,
had an enemy inflicted, she would scarcely have forgiven—
because she has prepared for him food which did not agree
with his constitution or habits.

And many a tender mother has, by pampering and incit-
ing the appetites of her young sons, laid the foundation of
their future course of selfishness and profligacy.

If the true principles of preparing food were understood,
these errors would not be committed, for the housekeeper
would then feel sure that the best food was that which best
nourished and kept the whole system in healthy action ; and
that such food would be best relished, because, whenever the
health is injured, the appetite is impaired or vitiated.   She
would no longer allow those kinds of food, which reason
and experience show are bad for the constitution, to appear
at her table.

Among those kinds of food which the good housekeeper
should scrupulously banish from her table, is that of *hot
leavened bread*.   From what I have seen, and from the nature of this almost indigestible food, when taken in large
quantities, I believe it more often lays the foundation of

diseases of the stomach, than any other kind of nourishment, used among us. Hot bread is eaten, morning and evening, at many of our city boarding-houses; and at establishments connected with the places of education for the young. And there it is, that that incipient disease, which terminates in *dyspepsia*, (an indefinable word implying almost every sort of distress and anguish to which the human frame is subject,) is often contracted. The want of sufficient exercise, or too strict attention to business or study, may, and no doubt does, have much influence in predisposing to this disease. But it is the *hot bread*, lying undigested, and of course *hard and heavy* in the stomach, which prostrates the system, and thus makes the mental fatigue injurious.

When much bodily exertion is used, in the open air, *hot bread*, as well as all other kinds of heavy food, is comparatively harmless. Hard-laboring people in the country, seldom suffer from indigestion. Still there are cases of disease, and the good housekeeper, even in the country, should beware of placing this food before her family. If you are out of bread, it is much better, both as regards economy and health, to bake an Indian cake by the fire, or make batter cakes, or even a short cake, if you do not put in too much butter, than to cut a *hot loaf from the oven*. Unleavened bread, when eaten warm, is more easily digested than leavened; or if, in the former, you use pearlash or sal æratus, it is still healthier.* Yet the best bread for constant use, is light, leavened bread from one to five or six days old. This may be toasted if you like variety. But do not, as you value the health and happiness of those who sit at your table, place before them hot leavened bread or biscuit.

Another kind of food, which ought to be banished from modern tables is *meat pies*. It seems strange that this kind of barbarous cookery should hold its place, since the introduction of so many excellent vegetables to eat with animal food; and since such substantial diet is not now required, as was needed when nearly all labor had to be performed

---

* In using pearlash or sal æratus, be careful not to put in too much. Some careless cooks dash in pearlash till their bread tastes as though it were wet with ley. This taste, if the *right* quantity only is used, will never be perceived.

by the physical strength of man. The Black Knight and Friar Tuck could take an enormous meal of venison pasty, washed down with wine, without any danger of injury, for their exercises in the open air, and the weight of armor which the knight bore, required this concentrated and stimulating food to sustain their strength; but now, when the modes of life have so far abated the muscular power of men, that it takes the united strength of five to lift a knight in armor into his saddle, would the same kind and quantity of food be beneficial?

Some may think that if this food were still as commonly eaten, men would now have more strength; but it would not be so, unless they used as much and as violent exercise in the open air, as was then the custom. It is only the *food that is digested* which gives strength, and really nourishes the system; when the mode of life is sedentary and confined, the powers of digestion are soon weakened, and we must adapt our diet to this condition of our nature. I have therefore entirely omitted receipts for meat pies; and though sometimes those who labor very hard may eat them without much danger, yet it would be more safe, as well as saving, to dress the meat by itself, and use vegetables and bread with it, rather than make it into a high-seasoned pie, with rich crust, a dish commonly eaten without vegetables.

Another improvement in this dietetic system of cookery is the entire exclusion of distilled spirits. I have not permitted the name of *rum* or *brandy* to sully a receipt in this book. There is no need of these as condiments; and though men may not be willing to relinquish their legal *right* to the use of such liquors, yet I cannot believe any man will regret their banishment from the cook's department. No father who deserves the name, can wish to have his children taught to love the taste of rum and brandy from having it mixed with their food.

If women will decidedly and entirely banish ardent spirits*

---

* Rum or brandy is used by some ladies as cosmetics to wash the face and hair, or as a remedy against colds, &c. to bathe the head and feet.

It is a very mistaken notion that these heating, drying liquids will make the hair grow—except it be to grow gray—or the complexion fair and smooth. There is always a sort of stickiness left on the from the household arrangements, (and they can do this if they choose,) the progress of true temperance habits would soon either make temperance laws unnecessary, or cause them to be respected and obeyed.

But the art of selecting and preparing food, or seeing that this is done by others, constitutes only a part of the good housekeeper's duty. She ought to understand the character and capacity of each member of her family, know how to assign, advantageously, the different kinds of work to her help, to calculate expenses, provide for exigencies, and remedy, as far as possible, all the mistakes and accidents which occur in her housekeeping.

Far the greater proportion of households, throughout our whole country, are managed without the aid of much hired help, by the females of each family. The maxim, " If you would be well served, you must serve yourself," has considerable truth in it ; at least those families who serve themselves, escape many vexations of spirit, because, if the work be not very well done, when we do it with our own hands, we are more apt to be satisfied. There are some sorts of domestic work, that of dairy work is one, which no hired help would be competent to discharge. This must be done by a wife or daughter, who feels a deep personal interest in the prosperity of her husband or father. Many of our farmers' wives are among the best housekeepers in the land, possessing that good sense, vigor of mind, native delicacy of taste or tact, and firm conscientiousness, which gift the

skin after washing in rum, which pure soft water never leaves. This stickiness closes the pores of the skin, and thus proves really injurious to its healthy action, and consequently beauty. I have known one example of this effect of rum, which was not at all favorable ; a lady, in consequence of a nervous affection in her jaw, had used rum for fourteen years to wash in—not a drop of water had touched her face or neck during that time. She was not very old, but her skin looked as dry and shrivelled as a baked sweet apple— you could scarcely put down a pin's point without touching a wrinkle.

In regard to the use of rum, brandy, &c. as a medicine, as far as my observation has extended, when considered as family remedies, *they never effect a cure.* Those persons who are in the habit of using them, always *require* them. If you wish to be well, and to have your family enjoy health, do not use rum or brandy in any way as medicines.

character with power to attempt every thing that duty demands. These are the "noble matronage" which our re-
public should honor; for it is the sons of such mothers who
have ever stood foremost to defend or serve their country—

"With word, or pen, or pointed steel."

One of the greatest defects in the present system of female
education, is the almost total neglect of showing the young
lady how to apply her learning so as to improve her domestic economy. It is true that necessity generally teaches, or
rather obliges her to learn this science after she is married;
but it would have saved her from many anxious hours, and
tears, and troubles, if she had learned how to make bread
and coffee, and cook a dinner before she left her father's
house; and it would have been better still, if she had been
instructed at school to regard this knowledge as an indispensable accomplishment in the education of a young lady.

I was once told by a lady of Boston that, when she was
married, she scarcely knew how a single dish should be prepared. The first day of her housekeeping, the cook came
for orders—"What would she have for dinner?"

The lady told her, among other items, that she would
have an apple pudding.

"How shall I make it?" was the question which the lady
was unable to answer—she knew no more how to make a
pudding than to square the circle. She evaded the question
as well as she could, by telling the girl to make it in the
usual way. But the circumstance was a powerful lesson on
the inconveniences of ignorance to the housekeeper. The
lady possessed good sense, and was a woman of right principles. She felt it was her duty to know how to order
her help—that wealth did not free her from responsibility
in her family. She set herself diligently to the study of
cookery; and, by consulting friends, watching the operations of her servants, and doing many things herself, she
has become a most excellent housekeeper.

For the young bride, who is entirely ignorant of her
household duties, this is an encouraging example; let her
follow it, if she would be happy and respected at home.
But it would be better to begin her lessons a little earlier;
it is not every woman who has sufficient strength of mind

to pursue such a rigid course of self-education. And no lady can be comfortable, unless she possess a knowledge of household work; if she need not perform it herself, she must be able to teach her help, otherwise she will always have *bad servants.*

I am aware that it is the fashion with many ladies to disparage Irish domestics, call them stupid, ignorant, impudent, ungrateful, the plagues of housekeeping. That they are ignorant, is true enough; it does require skill, patience, and judgment, to teach a raw Irish girl how to perform the work in a gentleman's family; but they are neither stupid nor ungrateful, and if they are taught in the right manner, they prove very capable, and are most faithful and affectionate domestics.

A friend of mine, who is just what a woman ought to be, capable of directing—even *doing*, if necessary—in the kitchen as well as shining in the drawing room, hired one of these poor despised Irish girls, new from the land of the Shamrock, who only understood the way of doing work in a hovel, yet, like all her class, she said, "Sure couldn't she do any thing the lady wanted?" The lady, however, did not trust the girl to make any experiments, but went to the kitchen with her, and taught her, or rather did the work herself, and allowed the *help* to look on and learn by example, which for such is much more effectual than lectures. When the dinner was nearly ready, the lady retired to dress, telling Julia to watch the roast, and she would return soon, and show her how to prepare it for the table. We may imagine with what utter bewilderment the poor girl had been overwhelmed during this, her first lesson in civilized life. The names of the articles of furniture in the kitchen, as well as their uses, were entirely unknown to her; and she had seen so many new things done, which she was expected to remember, that it must have made her heart-sick to reflect how much she had to learn. But there was one thing she thought she understood—which was to cook potatoes. These were done, and she would show the lady she knew how to prepare them for the table.

When the lady returned, she found the girl seated on the floor, the potatoes in her lap, while she, with a very satisfied look, was peeling them with her fingers!

Are there not ladies who would have exclaimed—"O, the stupid, ignorant, dirty creature! She cannot be taught to do my work. I must send her away!" And away she would have been sent, irritated if not discouraged, and perhaps without knowing a place where to lay down her head in this strange country.

My friend did not act in this manner—she expressed no surprise at the attitude of the girl, only quietly said—"That is not the best way to peel your potatoes, Julia—just lay them on this plate, and I will show you how I like to have them done."

That Irish girl remained a servant in the same family for five years, proved herself not only capable of learning to work, but willing and most devoted in the service of her mistress, whom she regarded with a reverence little short of what a Catholic feels for his patron saint.* And thus, if with

---

* Julia married before she left her mistress, and the manner in which that kind lady treated her on the occasion, will show the character of both.

It was late in the afternoon when Julia informed her mistress she must be married that same evening, because her intended husband was to start the next morning for the West.

"I will send for the Bishop, then, and have some cake and wine ready for you, Julia," said the lady.

"Thank you, ma'am—but I suppose I must be married in the church," replied Julia, who was a good Catholic.

"Then I will go and see you married," said the lady.

"Will you, will you do that same?" said Julia, with uplifted hands, her very pretty face sparkling with joy.

"Yes—and you must invite the Bishop (Cheverus) to return home with you, and partake of some cake and wine."

At the marriage, when the bride was to make her promises of faithfulness, obedience, &c. the Bishop inquired who would be her surety. In the Catholic marriage service, this sort of guaranty is required, like that of sponsors in baptism.

Julia had not thought of this; but her mistress was there, she came forward, saying to the Bishop—"I will be surety for Julia—she has been in our family five years, and has proved herself an excellent domestic; I will answer for her faithfulness as a wife."

"You are too kind!" exclaimed the Bishop, clasping his hands in thankfulness—and in his exhortation to the wedded pair, he reminded the bride how deeply she was indebted to her mistress, who had taught and directed her in the right way, and exhorted her to prove herself worthy, by continued good conduct, of such a generous friend. And Julia has done this—she is settled at the West, her husband a respectable mechanic, and she a good wife.

patience and kindness these poor Irish girls are treated and taught, may good and faithful help be obtained.

But unless ladies know how the work should be done, and are willing to teach their domestics, they should not employ the Irish when they first arrive.

Those who do employ and carefully instruct this class of persons, perform a most benevolent act to the usually desti-tute exiles, and also a good service to the community, by rendering those who would, if ignorant, become a burden and a nuisance, useful, and often respectable members of society.

To educate a good domestic is one of the surest proofs that a lady is a good housekeeper.

CHAPTER XV.

A WORD TO MOTHERS.

"Train up a child in the way he should go, &c."

To be known as a " good housekeeper"—in the compre-hensive sense of the term,—should secure to a woman high respect; but if you are a *mother*, the crowning grace of your household management will be, that you have rightly trained the children committed to your care.   Only bear in mind that the *first feeling* of the infant is desire for food, the *first pleasure* in life, the gratification of appetite, and we shall see of what immense importance it is that the habit of regulating this instinct for food by the rules of reason and experience should be the first one formed in our children. Of course, the foundation of this habit must be laid in the entire submission of the appetites of the young child to the reason and experience of its mother.

The kinds of food most proper for young children have been briefly noticed in this work.   But the regulation of the quantity and times of taking food are of the utmost

importance—this should be the mother's province.   There
is great danger that an infant, under three years of age, will
be over-fed, if it be left to the discretion of the nurse.
These persons, generally, have but one resource to stop the
screaming of a child, whether it proceed from pain, or cross-
ness, or repletion (as it often does)—they give it something
to eat—often that which is very injurious, to tempt the appetite; if it will only eat and stop crying, they do not care for
the future inconvenience which this habit of indulgence
may bring on the child and its mother.

Arrange, as early as possible, the regular times of giving
food to your children, according to their age and constitution.   But remember that all temperaments are not alike.
Some of the same age may require more food than others.
One rule, however, will apply to all—never give a child food
to amuse and keep it quiet when it is not hungry, or to re-
ward it for being good.   You may as rationally hope to
extinguish a fire by pouring on oil, as to cure a peevish temper or curb a violent one by pampering the appetite for luxuries in diet; and all the traits of goodness you thus seek
to foster will, in the end, prove as deceptive as the mirage
of green fields and cool lakes to the traveller in the hot
sands of the desert.

"My children have very peculiar constitutions," said an
anxious mother—"they are so subject to fevers!   If they
take the least cold, or even have a fall, they are sure to be
attacked by fever."   The family lived high, and those young
children had a seat at the table, and were helped to the best
and richest of every thing.   And their luncheon was cake
and confectionary.

It was suggested to the mother that if she would adopt a
different diet for those children, give them bread and milk
morning and evening, and a plain dinner of bread, meat and
vegetables, their liability to fevers would be much lessened.

"My children do not love milk, and won't touch plain
food"—was the answer, with a sort of triumphant smile,
as though this cramming of her children with good things
till the blood of the poor little creatures was almost in a
state of inflammation, was a high credit to her good house-
keeping.

But do not err on the .other hand; and for fear your child

should be over-fed, allow it insufficient nourishment. There is not in our country, much reason to fear that such will be the case; the danger is, usually, on the side of excess; still we must not forget that the effects from a system of slow starvation are, if not so suddenly fatal as that of repletion, more terrible, because it reduces the intellectual as well as the physical, nature of man, till he is hardly equal to the brutes.

In many parts of civilized and Christian Europe, the mass of the people suffer from being over-worked and under-fed; few may die of absolute starvation, but their term of life is much shortened, and their moral and intellectual powers dwarfed or prostrated.

"Under an impoverished diet," says Dr. Combe, "the moral and intellectual capacity is deteriorated as certainly as the bodily"—and he adverts to the work-house and charitable institution system of weak soups and low vegetable diet, and to the known facts that children brought up on such fare are usually feeble, puny and diseased in body, and are at best but moderate in capacity.

The rational course seems to be, to feed infants, till about three years old, chiefly with milk and mild farinaceous vegetable preparations; a large portion of good bread, light, well-baked, and *cold*, should be given them; after that period, to proportion their solid food to the amount of exercise they are able to take. Children who play abroad in the open air, will require more hearty nourishment, more meat, than those who are kept confined in the house or school-room. From the age of ten or twelve to sixteen or eighteen, when the growth is most rapid and the exercises (of boys especially) most violent, a sufficiency of plain nourishing food should be given; there is little danger of their taking too much, if it be of the right kind and properly cooked. But do not allow them to eat hot bread, or high-seasoned meats and rich gravies, or use any kind of stimulating drinks.

I feel sure that every sensible mother will be willing to dispense with all alcoholic preparations in cookery. There is no doubt that many a fair promising boy who has ended his life an intemperate man, had the taste for liquor first excited and fostered by seeing it used daily as a necessary in the family, and often tasting it in the richest and most savory kinds of food. What Christian mother will venture to teach, by her own example, the love of this moral and mental poison to her young children? If the family mode of living were " temperate in all things ;" with suitable bathings and recreations, very little sickness would occur among children ; and simple remedies would generally be found to relieve common attacks of disease. I shall give a few such remedies—those that are most easily to be obtained, and used chiefly for accidental injuries.

For Burns.—Apply cotton wool dipped in oil as soon as possible, and keep it on till the fire is entirely out, which will usually take from two days to a week.

For a Cut.—Wash off the blood in cold water, and bind it up with a clean cotton bandage ; if it inclines to bleed, put on scraped lint, after bringing the edges of the wound together as closely as possible, and bind it rather tight. Or use sticking plaster.

When a Nail or Pin has been run into the Foot, instantly bind on a rind of salt pork ; if the foot swell, bathe it in a strong decoction of wormwood, then bind on another rind of pork, and keep quiet till the wound is well. The lockjaw is often caused by such wounds, if neglected.

For a Bruise or Sprain.—Bathe the part in cold water, till you can get ready a decoction of wormwood. This is one of the best remedies for sprains and bruises. When the wormwood is fresh gathered, pound the leaves, and wet them either with water or vinegar, and bind them on the bruise ; when the herb is dry, put into it cold water, and let it boil a short time, then bathe the bruise, and bind on the herb.

For Chafes.—Apply cotton wool. Always keep cotton wool, scraped lint and wormwood on hand.

The Ear-ache is usually caused by a sudden cold. Steam the head over hot herbs, bathe the feet, and put into the ear cotton wool wet with sweet oil and paregoric.

For the Tooth-ache, if caused by a cold, a ginger poultice is the best remedy. Wet a thick flannel cloth in scalding vinegar, sprinkle it thickly over with ground ginger, and bind on the face when going to bed.

THE BEST PREVENTIVE OF COLDS is to wash your children every day thoroughly in cold water, if they are strong enough to bear it; if not, add a little warm water, and rub the skin dry. This keeps the pores open. If they do take cold, give them a warm bath as soon as possible; if that is not convenient, bathe the feet and hands, and wash the body all over in warm water, then give a cup of warm tea, and cover the patient in bed.

IF A SORE THROAT follow, take a tumbler of molasses and water, half and half, when going to bed; and rub the throat with a mixture of sweet or goose oil and spirits of turpentine, then wear a flannel round it.

FOR CANKER OR SORE MOUTH, steep blackberry leaves, sweeten with honey, sprinkle in a little burnt alum, and wash the mouth often with this decoction.

COOKERY FOR THE SICK.

The cookery for the sick requires great nicety and exactness, and should rarely be trusted to a common domestic. If you have a nurse constantly with your children, she may do this part of domestic duty well, otherwise it must generally devolve on the mother.

TO MAKE GRUEL.—Sift the Indian meal through a fine sieve; wet two spoonfuls of this meal with cold water, and beat it till there are no lumps; then stir it into a pint of boiling water, and let it boil half an hour, stirring it all the time.

BEEF TEA.—Cut half a pound of lean fresh beef into slices, lay it in a dish and pour over it a pint of boiling water, cover the dish and let it stand half an hour by the fire, then just boil it up, pour it off clear, and salt it very little.

VEAL TEA is made in the same way—and CHICKEN TEA also.

BARLEY WATER.—Upon one ounce of pearl, or common barley, after it has been well washed in cold water, pour half a pint of boiling water, and then boil it for a few minutes; the water must then be strained off and thrown away; afterwards a quart of boiling water must be poured over the barley; and which should then be boiled down to one pint and a quarter, and strained off. The barley water thus made is clear and mucilaginous; and when mixed with an equal quantity of good milk and a small portion of sugar, is an excellent substitute for the mother's milk, when infants are, unfortunately, to be brought up by hand. Without milk, it is one of the best beverages for all acute diseases, and may have lemon juice, raspberry vinegar, apple tea, infusion of tamarinds, or any other acidulous substance that is agreeable to the palate of the patient, mixed with it.

ARROW-ROOT forms an excellent nutritive mucilage. Put two tea-spoonfuls of the powder into a basin ; mix them smooth with a few tea-spoonfuls of cold water, and then let another person pour boiling water over the mixture while you continue to stir it, until it forms a kind of starchy-looking substance.

Arrow-root, thus prepared, may be used in the same manner as gruel. It is well adapted for the food of infants, because it is less liable to ferment than either gruel or barley-water ; and, for the same reason, it is the best fluid nourishment for those who are af flicted with diseases of indigestion. As it is very insipid, it requires either milk or wine, or acids, to be mixed with it, whichever may suit the taste and the state of habit of the person for whom it is intended. It forms an excellent pudding, when prepared like rice, for children who are a little beyond the age of infancy.

DECOCTION OF ICELAND LIVERWORT.—An ounce of liverwort must be carefully freed from the moss, fragments of stalks, and particles of dirt, with which it is frequently mixed, by rubbing it between the hands in cold water. Then steep it, for two hours, in such quantity of cold water as will completely cover it; after which it must be bruised, pounded, or cut, and the steeping continued for three or four days longer in a fresh quantity of boiling water, which, when the steeping is finished, must be strained off by pressure. The liverwort is then to be put into a quart of fresh water, and kept boiling until the fluid be reduced two thirds, or to a pint and a quarter. When strained and allowed to cool, it forms a thick mucilage, free from any bitter taste, and may be rendered very palatable by the addition of sugar and lemon juice; or by white wine, in those cases which permit the use of wine.

This decoction of liverwort is an excellent demulcent nutriment, in consumption, dysentery and in convalescence from acute diseases, and particularly after the hooping cough, in which case the bitter need not be completely removed, as it tends to invigorate the digestive organs.

FRESH CALF'S-FEET JELLY.—Scald, take off the hair, and wash very clean, four feet; put them into a sauce-pan with two quarts of cold water, and when it comes to boil, skim, then let them simmer for six hours; take out the feet and strain the liquor into a deep dish. The following day remove the fat carefully from the top, and give it another boil, till it is reduced to one quart of jelly. This may be flavored as you like. It must be dissolved and boiled again when seasoned. It is very delicate and nourishing for an invalid.

WINE WHEY.—Boil half a pint of milk, and pour as much sherry or other wine to it as will curdle it. Take the vessel off the fire, and when the curd sinks from off the whey, pour it off, sweeten it, and if too strong, add hot water to reduce it. *Vinegar Whey, Cream of Tartar, Lemon, Mustard-seed,* and *Alum Whey,* are all made in the same manner.

TOAST AND WATER.—Toast thin slices of bread on both sides carefully; then pour cold water over the bread and cover it tight for one hour; or use boiling water, and let it cool.

WATERS FOR COOLING DRAUGHTS *of Preserved or Fresh Fruits —Apple water—Lemon Water, &c.*—Pour boiling water on the preserved or fresh fruits, sliced; or squeeze out the juice, boil it with sugar, and add water.

BALM, MINT, AND OTHER TEAS.—These are simple infusions, the strength of which can only be regulated by the taste. They are made by putting either the fresh or the dried plants into boiling water in a covered vessel, which should be placed near the fire for an hour. The young shoots both of balm and of mint are to be preferred, on account of their strong aromatic qualities. These infusions may be drunk freely in feverish and in various other complaints, in which diluents are recommended. Mint tea, made with the fresh leaves, is useful in allaying nausea and vomiting.

CHAPTER XVI.

TRAITS OF DOMESTIC LIFE.

HIRING A COOK.

"If it were only a wife now, that I wanted, there would be some hope for me—but a cook!—Well, as it rains too hard for you, my love, to venture out, I must go," said Mr. Manning.

"I regret the necessity, my love, but this is the day; and if the woman does not hear from me, she will doubtless engage herself;—and she refuses to call here," replied Mrs. Manning.

How I wish we could have a patent invention for cooks as well as cooking stoves! thought Mr. Manning, as he entered the house where his intended cook resided.

She appeared—a large-formed, well-dressed female, with an air of much importance. In fashionable life she would have been what is called "a showy woman."

"Your terms are—"

"Three dollars a week, sir."

"That is more than we have been accustomed to give. My family is not large; five in the parlor, only; and we have a house maid and boy," said Mr. Manning.

" You may hire cooks cheaper, I suppose," said Madame Cook—
" that is my price."

" I will give you two dollars and a half—though we never have
paid over nine shillings."

" It is of no consequence to talk about it," said the woman, in-
dignantly : and she swept out of the room with a lofty gesture that
might have been a lesson to an insulted tragedy queen.

" Let me calculate," thought Mr. Manning, as he walked home.
" I cannot expect to realize more than fifteen hundred clear, from
the profits of my store—very likely it will be less. And now—$3
per week for a cook—$1,25 each for the boy and chambermaid—is
five dollars and a half per week. Then the board $2 each per week ;
it will cost all that at the present rate of provisions—$6—making
$11,50—or *five hundred and seventy-five* per year for help.

" Then for rent, provision, taxes, fuel, clothing, and all et ceteras
for myself and family, there remains $925—and my daughters want
masters, and my wife must, for her health, go one journey in a year.

" There must be something radically wrong in the present fashions of society. An educated man thinks it no shame to do the business of his profession, whatever it may be. I work hard in my
store every day. But women, who have been educated, think it de-
grading to put their hands to any household employment, though
that is all the task we assign to our females. A lady would be
ashamed to be seen in her kitchen at work. O, how many are now
sitting at ease in their pleasant parlors, while their husbands, fathers, brothers and sons are toiling like slaves ! And, what is worse
than toil, anxiously bearing a load of care, lest their income should
not, with all their exertions, be sufficient to meet the expenses of
their families.

" It cannot continue thus. If women who receive a fashionable
education are thereby rendered incapable of performing their domestic duties—why, an educated man must remain single till he
amasses a fortune—or must marry a *real help* in order to have a *help
meet* for him.

" Yet it may be the folly and pride of us men, after all. We
want the sole control of business and the whole credit of the pecu-
niary management of our households. We do not confide to our
wives and daughters the embarrassments we suffer, or the need we
have for their assistance—at least co-operation. I will tell my wife
and daughters precisely how my affairs stand."

The two elder Misses Manning (the youngest is at school) take
each her turn in the kitchen every other week, and with the counsel
of Mrs. Manning and the help of the boy and a washerwoman once
a week, every thing in the household department goes on like clock-
work. They declare they will never be at the trouble of attempting
to hire another cook. And what is still more agreeable, Mr. Manning avers that their table was never before so well arranged, or his
daughters so gay and contented for a month together ; and they say,
that they never had so much time for their music and studies.

Early rising and active employment, for a few hours each day, are
wonderful promoters of good health and cheerfulness ; leisure is

never appreciated till it is earned by efforts to be useful, or enjoyed as relaxation from that industry, which, in some way, is the duty of every national being.

THE GOOD DINNER.

" Be particular that the dinner is in the very best style, Ruth; and pray see yourself that the ducks' feet are crimped. I would not, for the universe, this should be forgotten, to-day. The feet are Mr. B——'s tit-bit," said Mrs. B. to a girl who acted as an upper domestic or sort of housekeeper. Mrs. B. strove, as much as possible, to imitate European customs.

Now it seemed very kind in the lady to think so much of her husband ; but domestics are shrewd observers, and soon learn the policy of the people with whom they live, and their respect is secured, or ridicule incurred, by the *motives* rather than the *results* of the family arrangement.

"Mrs. B. is intending to have some new finery, I guess," said Ruth to the cook, after she had given the directions about the dinner.

The truth was, Mrs. B. had been invited to a very select party of the fashionables ; she wished to outshine all the ladies, and a new dress and set of pearl ornaments were to be the price of the dinner in general, and the ducks' feet in particular.

Mr. B. was a great man on 'change, for he was rich ; and he was envied for the means of felicity he enjoyed at home ; surrounded by every comfort and luxury which wealth could purchase, or a bachelor require to make him happy. Mr. B. also possessed that crowning bliss, a handsome wife, who devoted herself to the dressing of her own pretty person and her husband's dinners, both in the very best style.

This style she thought the most important thing on earth. She had a nurse for the baby, a nursery maid for the two small children, a governess for her eldest daughter, and the son, a fine lad of twelve, was placed at a famous seminary for boys, where every thing necessary to perfect him in the manners of a gentleman was taught— as his mother said. What time had a fashionable mother to devote to the education of her children ? And what duty had she to fulfil save to provide fashionable teachers ? It was for the poor and the plebeian to spend their days and nights in the nursery.

Were Mr. and Mrs. B. happy ? You shall judge. The sumptuous dinner is on the table, diffusing, through the luxurious apartment, its savory odors.

" You are five minutes too late with your dinner to-day," said Mr. B. sourly.

" I know it, my love," said Mrs. B. in a most sweet tone; " but the cook is so slow."

" I wish you would send her away then, and have one who will do things in season," said Mr. B.

" She does her work very well, my love."

" Sometimes too well, my dear—this beef is roasted to rags."

"Now pray try the ducks, my love."

"Umph!"

A long pause on both sides succeeded this emphatic "umph!"
Mr. B. was occupied in tasting (for appetite to eat he had not) the
various rich dishes. It was an anxious period for Mrs. B. She
watched her husband's countenance as he scrutinized the ducks'
feet. They were crimped beautifully—but "the full soul loathes
the honeycomb." Mr. B. had not digested his late supper of the
previous evening, or his rich toast and mutton chop of the morning
meal, or his twelve o'clock lunch. He felt the desire to eat, but
alas! the oppression of his stomach seemed like the weight of an
incubus, and took from him all power of gratifying his propensity.
He suddenly turned from the ducks' feet without a single compli-
ment to his wife. Tears swelled in her eyes—not that her husband
had lost his appetite, but that she should lose her pearls.

Mr. B. considered his wife and children as persons for whom he
was bound to provide. Mrs. B. thought of her husband as one
for whom she must arrange her table. Neither of them had ever
purposed to make their home the place of happiness and improvement for themselves and children. There was no companionship in
their pursuits. He disliked large parties, as men of sense and business usually do. She delighted in large parties, because she had no
other pursuit but fashion and show. She soon had the sagacity to
discover that her husband's consent to the expense and parade of a
party was easier to be won feasting than fasting. Like the Boa
Constrictor when gorged, he could be managed. So she graduated
her *cuisine* to the degree she intended to operate on his patience and
purse, and she usually succeeded. These triumphs had been bought
only at the expense of her husband's health : but as that suffered, she
had found to her sorrow, her influence decayed, and that the black
melancholy which a disordered digestion so often produces, caused
him to be irascible, morose, tyrannical even.

We never do wrong, never violate nature's laws without paying
the penalty. The first sin was yielding to the temptation of eating that which
seemed good ; and woman gained her first victory over the reason
of man by tempting his appetite. This reason has never been un-
clouded since, and never will be till she learns to awaken some
better and nobler feeling, than the indulgence of appetite in him, as
the medium of companionship with herself.

The prevalence of *intemperance in eating*, of luxury in living, is
more the fault of woman than of man. She is the guardian of home;
she can regulate the arrangement of her household : she can form
the habits of her children ; she does form them. Shall we wonder
that men are selfish and luxurious, while they are taught, by their
mothers or nurses, from their cradles to consider the indulgence of
appetite—eating those things which *taste good*,—as the greatest privilege and happiness which can be enjoyed?

"Just as the twig is bent, the tree's inclined."

A CATALOG OF SELECTED
DOVER BOOKS
IN ALL FIELDS OF INTEREST

A CATALOG OF SELECTED DOVER

BOOKS IN ALL FIELDS OF INTEREST

CONCERNING THE SPIRITUAL IN ART, Wassily Kandinsky. Pioneering work by father of abstract art. Thoughts on color theory, nature of art. Analysis of earlier masters. 12 illustrations. 80pp. of text. 5⅜ × 8½.   23411-8 Pa. $3.95

ANIMALS: 1,419 Copyright-Free Illustrations of Mammals, Birds, Fish, Insects, etc., Jim Harter (ed.). Clear wood engravings present, in extremely lifelike poses, over 1,000 species of animals. One of the most extensive pictorial sourcebooks of its kind. Captions. Index. 284pp. 9 × 12.   23766-4 Pa. $12.95

CELTIC ART: The Methods of Construction, George Bain. Simple geometric techniques for making Celtic interlacements, spirals, Kells-type initials, animals, humans, etc. Over 500 illustrations. 160pp. 9 × 12. (USO)   22923-8 Pa. $9.95

AN ATLAS OF ANATOMY FOR ARTISTS, Fritz Schider. Most thorough reference work on art anatomy in the world. Hundreds of illustrations, including selections from works by Vesalius, Leonardo, Goya, Ingres, Michelangelo, others. 593 illustrations. 192pp. 7⅛ × 10¼.   20241-0 Pa. $9.95

CELTIC HAND STROKE-BY-STROKE (Irish Half-Uncial from "The Book of Kells"): An Arthur Baker Calligraphy Manual, Arthur Baker. Complete guide to creating each letter of the alphabet in distinctive Celtic manner. Covers hand position, strokes, pens, inks, paper, more. Illustrated. 48pp. 8¼ × 11.
24336-2 Pa. $3.95

EASY ORIGAMI, John Montroll. Charming collection of 32 projects (hat, cup, pelican, piano, swan, many more) specially designed for the novice origami hobbyist. Clearly illustrated easy-to-follow instructions insure that even beginning papercrafters will achieve successful results. 48pp. 8¼ × 11.   27298-2 Pa. $2.95

THE COMPLETE BOOK OF BIRDHOUSE CONSTRUCTION FOR WOOD-WORKERS, Scott D. Campbell. Detailed instructions, illustrations, tables. Also data on bird habitat and instinct patterns. Bibliography. 3 tables. 63 illustrations in 15 figures. 48pp. 5¼ × 8½.   24407-5 Pa. $1.95

BLOOMINGDALE'S ILLUSTRATED 1886 CATALOG: Fashions, Dry Goods and Housewares, Bloomingdale Brothers. Famed merchants' extremely rare catalog depicting about 1,700 products: clothing, housewares, firearms, dry goods, jewelry, more. Invaluable for dating, identifying vintage items. Also, copyright-free graphics for artists, designers. Co-published with Henry Ford Museum & Green-field Village. 160pp. 8¼ × 11.   25780-0 Pa. $9.95

HISTORIC COSTUME IN PICTURES, Braun & Schneider. Over 1,450 costumed figures in clearly detailed engravings—from dawn of civilization to end of 19th century. Captions. Many folk costumes. 256pp. 8⅜ × 11¾.   23150-X Pa. $11.95

THE INFLUENCE OF SEA POWER UPON HISTORY, 1660–1783, A. T. Mahan. Influential classic of naval history and tactics still used as text in war colleges. First paperback edition. 4 maps. 24 battle plans. 640pp. 5⅜ × 8½.
25509-3 Pa. $12.95

THE STORY OF THE TITANIC AS TOLD BY ITS SURVIVORS, Jack Winocour (ed.). What it was really like. Panic, despair, shocking inefficiency, and a little heroism. More thrilling than any fictional account. 26 illustrations. 320pp. 5⅜ × 8½. 20610-6 Pa. $8.95

FAIRY AND FOLK TALES OF THE IRISH PEASANTRY, William Butler Yeats (ed.). Treasury of 64 tales from the twilight world of Celtic myth and legend: "The Soul Cages," "The Kildare Pooka," "King O'Toole and his Goose," many more. Introduction and Notes by W. B. Yeats. 352pp. 5⅜ × 8½. 26941-8 Pa. $8.95

BUDDHIST MAHAYANA TEXTS, E. B. Cowell and Others (eds.). Superb, accurate translations of basic documents in Mahayana Buddhism, highly important in history of religions. The Buddha-karita of Asvaghosha, Larger Sukhavativyuha, more. 448pp. 5⅜ × 8½. 25552-2 Pa. $9.95

ONE TWO THREE . . . INFINITY: Facts and Speculations of Science, George Gamow. Great physicist's fascinating, readable overview of contemporary science: number theory, relativity, fourth dimension, entropy, genes, atomic structure, much more. 128 illustrations. Index. 352pp. 5⅜ × 8½. 25664-2 Pa. $8.95

ENGINEERING IN HISTORY, Richard Shelton Kirby, et al. Broad, nontechnical survey of history's major technological advances: birth of Greek science, industrial revolution, electricity and applied science, 20th-century automation, much more. 181 illustrations. ". . . excellent . . ."—Isis. Bibliography. vii + 530pp. 5⅜ × 8¼.
26412-2 Pa. $14.95

Prices subject to change without notice.

Available at your book dealer or write for free catalog to Dept. GI, Dover Publications, Inc., 31 East 2nd St., Mineola, N.Y. 11501. Dover publishes more than 500 books each year on science, elementary and advanced mathematics, biology, music, art, literary history, social sciences and other areas.